Robert V Dodge

CATHERINE CATER

CATHERINE CATER

An Elegant Rise Above Race and Gender as Scholar and Professor

ROBERT V. DODGE

Algora Publishing
New York

Library of Congress Cataloging-in-Publication Data —

Names: Dodge, Robert, 1945– author.
Title: Catherine Cater: An Elegant Rise Above Race and Gender as Scholar
and Professor / Robert V. Dodge.
    Description: New York : Algora Publishing, [2016] | Includes bibliographical
    references and index.
    Identifiers: LCCN 2016030980 (print) | LCCN 2016031384 (ebook) | ISBN
    9781628942132 (soft cover : alk. paper) | ISBN 9781628942149 (hard cover :
    alk. paper) | ISBN 9781628942156 (pdf)
    Subjects: LCSH: Cater, Catherine, 1917–2015. | College teachers—United
    States—Biography. | Racially mixed people—United States—Biography. |
    North Dakota State University—Faculty—Biography. | North Dakota
State
    University—History—20th century.
    Classification: LCC LA2317.C375 D64 2016 (print) | LCC LA2317.C375
(ebook) |
    DDC 378.1/25092 [B] —dc23
    LC record available at https://lccn.loc.gov/2016030980

Cover painting "When I Grow Up," by Lourdes Hawley

Printed in the United States

For Mya and Tai Carroll Carpenter

ACKNOWLEDGEMENTS

I would like to thank Jane Dodge and Mike Morrissey for their reading of this manuscript and their helpful suggestions. The North Dakota State University Archives in Fargo, North Dakota, warrants mention for the supportive access provided to its Catherine Cater Collection. My appreciation also to Chantel Clark, the Special Collections Librarian at Fisk University, for her assistance in locating the Catherine Cater materials in their archives. I would also like to express my gratitude to those who knew Catherine Cater and contributed by allowing me to interview them regarding their recollections. This includes Yvonne Condell, Greg Danz, Stephen Disrud, Peggy Gaynor, Lourdes Hawley, Paul Homan, Don Larew, Mike Morrissey, Jerry Richardson, Lou Richardson, Ene Kõivastik Vogel, and Steve Ward. Helpful correspondence that deserves my appreciative recognition came from Kevin Carvelle, William (Bill) Cosgrove, John Cox, Laura McDaniel, Thomas Riley, and Pat Stocker. My final expression of gratitude is to Andrea Sengstacken and her fellow editors at Algora Publishing for their professionalism in the production of this book.

TABLE OF CONTENTS

PREFACE

This is the story of Catherine Cater, a distinguished teacher and intellectual who had an infectious love of ideas. English literature and philosophy were her primary scholarly areas, but her curiosity knew no bounds. Her heritage was Southern and most of her ancestors came from Georgia. Catherine was born in New Orleans, then spent her youth in Alabama. Diverse influences that varied from experiences with the Ku Klux Klan to immersion in Great Books came together in the creation of this enigma who was an eminent and influential woman. Dr. Cater faced barriers of race and gender when she entered the academic world and moved to the North, but she elevated the level of scholarship at universities and their communities in both the South and North. Most notable was North Dakota State University in Fargo, North Dakota, where she spent the major portion of her long career, and left an indelible mark on the academic stature of the institution.

There are inconsistencies in this book regarding usage that are intentional and will be explained in the following paragraphs. On inconsistencies regarding terminology regarding capitalization and selection of terms related to race: While African-American is frequently used as a designation, I have used Black primarily and capitalized it as a term of racial reference. I have similarly capitalized White. While it is more common usage to use lower case letters for these words, this follows the style of historian Peggy Pascoe, who was a leader in her work on race in America. She explained in the introduction to *What Comes Naturally: Miscegenation Law and the Making of Race in America* (New York: Oxford University Press, 2010) that she hoped to broaden the word "Black" into something beyond a physical description and encompass a whole range of a widespread and diverse group of men and women of various skin colors and backgrounds, similar to capitalizing "Chinese" or "Japanese" for the residents and diaspora of those countries. Pascoe explains capitalizing White to mark what has often been an unmarked group and identify it as a group when it has been commonly taken as the norm in society. My inconsistencies in the capitalization that frequently show up are when language comes from documents or direct quotes that have been preserved without such capitalization. There is frequent use of the word Negro to refer to Black Americans that comes from the time and the people who identified themselves with that word. Exceptions are in direct quotations.

Author with Catherine Cater, May 22, 2012

The telling of the story may appear unusual or uneven. That is due to the author's relationship with the subject of this book. The author was Catherine Cater's student over 50 years ago and remained her friend from that time onward. In telling her story, he has blended first-person recollection with third-person narration based on research and interviews. Hopefully, adding the memories of personal encounters with this woman will help bring her to life as the real person she was and convey a better understanding of why she is so highly regarded by those who benefitted from having been in her presence.

CHAPTER 1. INTRODUCTION

It was the fall of 1963 when I began my freshman year at North Dakota State University. As a Fargo native, staying home where the school was located, I wasn't very excited about being there. A number of my high school friends headed off to distant colleges, and many of those who had remained and enrolled at "Moo U" (as the former North Dakota Agricultural College was derisively called) had joined fraternities, which I had chosen not to consider. There was a contrived social division among students at the time. It was based on those who joined fraternities and sororities, the Greek system, as an artificial elite, and those who were not accepted, or chose not to attempt to participate, the "independents." Between members of the Greek system and the independents, there existed somewhat of a feeling of mutual superiority, and I shared that with the independents. The Gold Star Band was my solace; Putnam Hall, where music was housed, was a place of welcome and camaraderie; and the student union soon became a second abode for escape.

My life at Fargo Central High had been one of involvement in activities while "getting by" in the classroom. My parents' very healthy attitude was to accept this while hoping I would maintain a B average to keep automobile insurance rates down. That was achieved, but studying was never something I allowed to interfere much with activities, though I had a fine history teacher my senior year, Richard Olson, who inspired some interest in listening to a scholar present material.

There was a general air of excitement around the campus that fall, because Darrell Mudra had come to town as both Head Football Coach and Athletic Director at North Dakota State, following the previous year's 0–10 disaster of a season. He had brought in a new staff and had recruited players that gave students and alumni hope for an escape from humiliation. During registration I had listed my intended major as "pre-med," and that fall I attended math and chemistry classes without great enthusiasm—though even less appealing was the mandatory Army Reserve Officer Training Corps (ROTC) with Sergeant Gromaski, a course that all U.S. male citizens were required to attend during their first two years. I was especially halfhearted about being present on drill days when we were required to attend school in uniform.

Enter English 101, Freshman English, where I had the great fortune to have been assigned to a section taught by Dr. Catherine Cater. As luck would have it, during the second quarter I was again assigned to Dr. Cater's Freshman English course, and my life was to be permanently changed.

As the winter quarter proceeded, the experience in her class remained consistent. We were a group of perhaps twenty-five or so students, mainly eighteen-year-olds, from around North Dakota, at an institution that prided itself on agriculture and engineering while offering a range of other options. We sat in our desks in an upper floor of Minard Hall, a three-story brick building in the southwest corner of the campus. Each day a somewhat diminutive woman would sweep, rather than walk, through the door at the front of the room and head straight to the window nearest where she would be standing when class started. She would grasp the wooden frame that held the large plate of glass and lean back as she struggled to open it, saying with what was almost a chuckle, "Air. We need some air!" That achieved, she would turn and look at us with her ever-present smile on her face and pause briefly.

At the time I addressed her as "Dr. Cater," as did all in our class. Dr. Cater was immediately fascinating, before she spoke. The image I recall of her is in loose sweaters, lavender, with her kinky hair cropped short, and an exotic look on her face that was dominated by her smile that exuded happiness, which I soon found beautiful. Her age was unclear but her energy made her seem young.

It was time to begin. We had an anthology, and our regular procedure was to receive reading assignments in advance, usually short stories, and then write essays on our reactions to what we had read. The only essay I can remember writing was entitled "The Circumstances That Swatted the Gadfly," after an assignment involving Socrates. The anthology wasn't easy, and all I can recall over 50 years later is James Joyce's "Araby," T.S. Eliot's "The Love Song of J. Alfred Prufrock," and Socratic dialogues by Plato.

Our essays prepared us for the discussion that constituted our class period. Dr. Cater would say something unthreatening, like: "Mr. Johnson [or someone], did you enjoy the reading?" And he/she might reply "Yes," which would bring an elated response, "Good, good!" or "Wonderful!" with the follow-up, "And what was it you enjoyed about it?" This is where she would work her magic.

Whatever was said, she could find something useful in it, some germ of an idea that could be related to the great thinkers of all history, and make that connection with enthusiasm and clarity. She would then call on someone else and do the same thing, nearly gushing over the response before restating it as another great thinker's view and making the person who had expressed it feel proud. Soon people would be contributing, discussing; and throughout it all she maintained control, as she took all comments and elevated them to brilliant ideas.

If a character in a story we had been assigned had made a choice to do something that could be described as virtuous or moral, the conversation might go as follows:

One student might comment, "I thought he did it because he was a good person."

Dr. Cater would excitedly respond, "Yes, yes, excellent! The very point Aristotle makes in his *Nicomachean Ethics*, where he spoke of virtuous actions stemming from virtuous character." She would explain further, "and as he noted, it is what the person with practical wisdom would choose."

Then the next person would add, "I guess he did a good thing, but really all you can do is try. I mean, this is a story, not the real world."

Once again, "Yes, yes, yes!" from Dr. Cater. "How very perceptive. Just as Epictetus and the Stoics would have it. The wise man will do what he can, but will have no regrets if tragedy results, as everything is governed by divine providence, and that course cannot be changed."

Next another, who objected to the idea of divine providence, would say, "What if everybody doesn't think the same, or agree on divine providence?"

Dr. Cater, again, would be extremely excited by this perceptive query. She'd reply, "Why, yes, yes! What a thoughtful question. It was very much what led Immanuel Kant to derive his categorical imperative. Kant said that in choosing actions, one should act only on rules that could be generalized to universal law." She would then proceed to carry on with a bit more explanation.

Interspersed at random in this discussion she would throw in quotations, likely to enhance our appreciation for the use of language, as she laughed softly. Two I recall were, "I should have been a pair of ragged claws/ Scuttling across the floors of silent seas," and "I have measured out my life with coffee spoons." Both are from T.S. Eliot's "The Love Song of J. Alfred Prufrock."

To an outsider who only observed the students' comments, this would appear to be a rather ordinary group, making statements that lacked any unusual perception. To those of us participating, it seemed an extremely invigorating discussion that involved a highly intellectual exchange of ideas in a scholarly forum. Everyone felt pride after each comment and energized after the class, as if we were something special, carrying on such an academic exchange.

In 1977 the *Spectrum*, the weekly paper of North Dakota State University, published a story about Dr. Cater that may have said it best. Ellen Kosse wrote of Catherine Cater, "Her manner and way of speaking can best termed in one word: elegant."[1]

At the end of July 2015, Catherine Cater passed away and left

---

1 Ellen Kosse, "Cater: 'infect one another with the desire to learn,' " *Spectrum* (NDSU), Feb 8, 1977, 6.

behind this simple statement that appeared in the Fargo *Forum* on August 1.[1]

Dear Friends,

Please permit me to leave quietly, without ceremony or ado. I thank you for the diverse ways in which each of you has contributed to my happiness and well-being. You have stimulated my thinking, cared about my feelings, and allowed me to be myself. What more can one ask of a life?

Thank you,
Catherine Cater

This appeal was quintessentially Catherine in its eloquence and its promotion of further inquiry. She had written this several years earlier, when there was no indication death was imminent.[2] All of us who knew her were diminished by her passing. A great teacher and friend had left us and our lives were reduced in richness and the loss of her insightful, uplifting company. That ever-present smile and inspiring intellect that graced our lives had vanished. Catherine's wishes were honored and she departed quietly.

Time has passed and she is now a part of history. There were many diverse influences that came together in molding this elegant woman, and they flowered so memorably during her years in Fargo. How this unique person became such a treasure and ended up in Fargo, North Dakota, was a mystery to me when we became friends during my college years. I was mainly thankful that somehow, she did. Our friendship continued from then on to the time she passed, and unraveling some of her story has only reinforced the great admiration I have always held for the most significant educator in my life.

---

1 Julie Sandland email to John Cox, forwarded to Robert Dodge, "I saw this in the Forum this morning and wanted to share with those of you who may not see it. It is a final farewell from Catherine Cater, very classic Catherine - full of clarity and wisdom in a few words." Aug 1, 2015.
2 Paul Homan interview with Robert Dodge, Fargo, ND, October 13, 2015.

As one of many whose lives were altered by being both a student and a friend of Catherine Cater, I record her legacy so that those who knew her can better understand her and relive fond memories and those who did not can have a glimpse of a great lady who once graced the campus of North Dakota State University.

CHAPTER 2. HERITAGE DISCLOSED

Dr. Cater became Catherine to me once I graduated and left North Dakota State. We remained friends from that time onward. To those who knew Catherine Cater well, as well as those who had only met her, it was common to wonder about her heritage from the time she arrived at North Dakota State University. There was something unusual about her appearance. I had immediately noticed her tightly curled hair, but that was insignificant because her piercing eyes focused intently on the person to whom she was speaking, and the mouth that so frequently broke into a smile evoking sincere joy dominated her appearance. Still, there was something in her look that was not "North Dakota." Could she be. . . ? In 1960, shortly before Catherine moved to North Dakota State University, or NDSU, the state of North Dakota had just 899 African-Americans in its population of 632,446.[1] Catherine's skin was perhaps a bit dusky, but certainly not dark, so there was no obvious reason to make assumptions.

Those who were included in the circle of Catherine's closest friends, regular visitors and confidants, in later years, had questions about her ethnicity. One was Mike Morrissey. Mike's route to Catherine's inner circle had a circuitous beginning. He came from a blue-collar background in Valley City, North Dakota, and

---

1 Quintard Taylor, *In Search of the Racial Frontier: African Americans in the American West 1528-1990* (New York: W. W. Norton, 1999), 279.

he first came to NDSU to get a "practical" degree. In the days of enrolment by arena scheduling, waiting in line and picking up class cards until they ran out, he first decided he would register in pharmacy. By the time his name came up, there were no cards remaining. Someone suggested electrical engineering as an alternative, so that became his major for his first two years. He then took an interest inventory at the counseling center and it indicated liberal arts might be a better match for him, and he took a course from John Hove on the American Short Story, which was the turning point for him. Mike became an English major and after his bachelor's degree, went on to receive his master's degree in English. It was at this time he studied with Catherine; later as a graduate teaching assistant he found himself sharing office space with her. They became friends and he remained among her close companions for the next 50 years.[1]

Mike notes his early lack of certainty about her ethnicity, recalling, "I don't think that when I first met Catherine that she strongly identified herself as a Black person. I think you had to read between the lines as she began to reveal parts about herself, about her father, losing her mother at a young age and living with her aunt on the south side of Chicago, that one came to know Catherine as a Black person."[2] In a comment, the first part of which would be later mirrored by one who held Catherine in a less favorable light, Mike added, "She certainly could have easily passed for White if she had wanted to, and she may have at some point, but I don't think I could have judged that . . . I didn't think about it. She was just a brilliant woman."[3]

Another in Catherine's intimate circle was Paul Homan. Paul came to NDSU from Kansas as a French teacher in the early 1980s. When Catherine retired, the honors program, known as the Scholars Program, that she had organized and implemented was moved from the English Department where she taught to Modern Languages. After brief interim directors, Paul took over the program, though Catherine remained involved, and the two worked together closely and developed great mutual admira-

---

1 Mike Morrissey, interview with Robert Dodge, Fargo, ND, Oct 9, 2015.
2 Ibid.
3 Ibid.

tion. He was among her closest confidants in her later years. As to wondering whether Catherine might be African-American, he commented, "I think everybody did. That was just another thing she never talked about. I don't know why. She sure didn't, ever, to my knowledge. I think a lot of people wondered about that, but you can't really speculate because there seemed to be no clues."[1]

Secretiveness and privacy were certainly qualities Catherine brought with her when she moved to the Fargo area, and she nurtured them well. They added to her mystique as someone all could engage with in conversation and the world of ideas, but who would always have a hint of mystery, perhaps beyond the realm of others (which was clearly the case). It was only during my final visit with her on June 11, 2015, the month before her passing, that her protective "invisibility cloak" was abandoned. After we had sat for some time enjoying conversation, she walked to a closet and pulled out a box that she brought over and opened. She withdrew a stack of old photographs of her family; we went through them slowly, as she identified her grandfather, father, uncles and aunts, a brother. All doubt about whether Catherine's heritage included African-Americans were eliminated.

With her passing and entering the world of historical figures, a look at her past makes it understandable why she might have chosen to leave it behind. It also sheds light on how she came to be the remarkable person she was, and how she came to adopt the attitudes and ideas she did. One can only admire her even more after an exploration of her heritage, yet questions also arise.

It is a fair conclusion from the earliest records available that Catherine's ancestors in early nineteenth-century Georgia were slaves.

The earliest record of Catherine's ancestry is of her great-grandfather on her father's side, who was named Cater, and whose wife's name had been Toole. According to their son's census record they both came from Georgia and were mulattoes.[2]

---

1 Paul Homan, interview with Robert Dodge, Fargo ND, Oct 13, 2015.
2 *Tenth Census of the United States*, 1880. (NARA microfilm publication T9, 1,454 rolls). Records of the Bureau of the Census, Record Group 29.

On her great-grandmother's side, she descended from Jack Tate, who was born in Virginia in 1840, and Jennie, born in Georgia in 1845. Jack and Jennie's daughter, Mary, was born in Alabama in 1864.[1] All these family members were listed as Black by the census taker.[2] The family can be traced from this point but the movement between states is indicative of sales. While Jack and Jennie's daughter Mary's middle initial appears variously as A, E, and O, this can be attributed to the handwritten records and transcriptions of the writing, as they are in references to the daughter of the same parents. Mary A is the most common name for the woman who would become Catherine's grandmother.

Stable families were not common among slaves in the antebellum South. The names appear to be accurate, as they are repeated in documents, though no record of marriages are included. The nature of the original relationships of the grandparents remains uncertain, since forced breeding was endemic in the slave community at that time as a way to increase the supply of slaves.[3] Women were listed as heads of families and valued for their ability to reproduce, while fathers were commonly not involved in family and childrearing. As a former slave testified, "If a man is big, good breed, dey gives him four, five women."[4]

Georgia was home for Catherine's ancestors for the second half of the nineteenth century and beyond. Records show their racial determination as somewhat murky, though that would have been of no significance in days preceding the Thirteenth Amendment in 1865 and the end of slavery. Georgia's slave codes applied equally to those who were part White, and to Blacks who were part Indian.[5] While later records would vary, most of

National Archives, Washington, District 567, Henry, Georgia; Roll: 152; Family History Film: 1254152; Page: 240D; Enumeration District: 070; Image: 0483.
1 *Tenth Census of the United States*, 1880. (NARA microfilm publication T9, 1,454 rolls). Records of the Bureau of the Census, Record Group 29. National Archives, Washington, D.C. Seale, Russell, Alabama; Roll: 30; Family History Film: 1254030; Page: 577A; Enumeration District: 158; Image: 0557.
2 Ibid.
3 Daina Berry, *Swing the Sickle for the Harvest is Ripe: Gender and Slavery in Antebellum Georgia* (Champaign, Ill: University of Illinois Press, 2007), 83.
4 Ibid.
5 Donald Grant, *The Way It Was in the South: The Black Experience in Georgia*

Catherine's ancestors would be classified as "mulattoes." In the South, for those of mixed race, it was the African ancestry that governed a person's status and fate. Legally this was first determined in the 1656 Virginia case *In re. Mulatto*, that ruled, "Mulatto held to be a slave and appeal taken."[1]

Soon after this case the Virginia legislature established another enduring precedent for the South. In 1662, 43 years after Africans were first brought to America as slaves, a law was passed that recognized that interracial sex occurred between White men and Black women, but with the 1662 law, White men were absolved of all consequences for the results of that interaction. Abandoning English common law where the children follow the status of the father, the Virginia law stated, "[C]hildren got by an Englishman upon a negro woman . . . shall be held bond or free only according to the condition of the mother."[2] The road was opened for White masters and their family members to demand sex from Black slave women, who had no recourse but to keep any children that resulted and raise them as slaves. This resulted in many mulattoes being born into slavery.

Catherine's grandfather was likely born into slavery and freed when he was nine; he died when Catherine was a two-year-old. Stories of the experiences these people endured were likely passed down from one generation to the next and can be assumed to have been common fare for family discussion in Catherine's early years with her father and his siblings. These memories persisted, and as Donald Grant writes, "As late as 1940 [when Catherine was in her 20s] it was still possible to find blacks whose parents or grandparents had remembered life in Africa and passed these recollections on as part of the oral tradition."[3]

Much is made of our forefathers' coming to America as the land of opportunity and the early settlers' proclaiming this a new land built on new principles as they escaped the persecution of Europe.

(Athens, GA: University of Georgia Press, 2001), 52.

1 Christine B. Hickman, "The Devil and One Drop Rule: Racial Categories, African Americans, and the U.S. Census," *Michigan Law Review*, Vol. 95, No. 5, Mar 1994, 1175.

2 Kevin R. Johnson, *Mixed Race and the Law*, New York: NYU Press, 2003, 105.

3 Grant, *The Way It Was in the South*, 44.

It is important to remember that a very different story exists for a significant portion of the population, that portion that did not choose to come here. A total of nearly 15 million Africans[1] were forcibly displaced and came to the Americas not for opportunity, but as chattel, property to be bought and sold at their owners' pleasure.

Though Catherine's great-grandfather's son believed his father was born in Georgia, he could conceivably have come from Africa. If not, her great-great grandparents certainly could have, and these may well have been stories in the Cater family's oral tradition that were a part of Catherine's youth. It would be a tradition for which most of us could not truly have empathy, but we should attempt to have sympathy since it is a part of our nation's story that this was done after declaring a belief in human equality. Great inhumanity was involved in what has come to be described in most histories as the "triangle trade." Europeans built forts on the west coast of Africa, and European traders brought textiles, rum, and guns to trade for human cargo. Tribal warfare and raiding was exploited and Africans exchanged captives for European goods. The merchants constrained potential slaves in caravans and shackled them, forcing them to walk sometimes up to 1,000 miles to coastal forts where they were put in underground dungeons until eventually boarding ships. Only half survived the marches,[2] and the most formidable challenge of their journey still lay ahead.

This was the "Middle Passage," where the cargo ships were loaded with slaves to be transported across the Atlantic to the Americas and the Caribbean islands. While it was normally a 60- to 90-day passage, there were times it was much longer. During this voyage the slaves were packed in incredibly crowded conditions below the deck, and men were commonly chained together in pairs. Women were often victims of sexual assault. The slaves were usually forced to lie on their backs with their heads between each other's legs, often in feces, urine, and blood when dysentery struck. Smallpox and yellow fever often became rampant in these conditions. Sometimes those who became ill were thrown over-

---

1 Philip D. Curtin, *The Atlantic Slave Trade: A Census* (Madison, WI: University of Wisconsin Press, 1972), 5.
2 "The African Slave Trade and the Middle Passage," *PBS*, http://www.pbs.org/wgbh/aia/part1/1narr4.html.

board to prevent further spread of infection. Between one and two million died during the crossing, and the living were often left chained to the dead until the ship's surgeon had the corpses thrown overboard.[1] The perils of the crossing were great and others committed suicide by jumping overboard when they had time on deck. There was so much death on the Middle Passage "that sharks regularly followed slave ships across the Atlantic."[2]

Once they arrived, the surviving slaves were exchanged for raw materials from the Americas and the Caribbean. Then they were sold at auction, while the ship and its crew headed back to Europe to exchange the new cargo for materials to take to Africa. This triangular cycle was repeated roughly 54,000 times,[3] buying and selling slaves.[4]

Slavery developed in all the British colonies of North America, but it only survived in those that would be called the South. Georgia, where the Cater family lived, was later than most in adopting a formal policy on slavery. The Georgia Assembly met in 1748 and drew up a slave code that became effective on January 1, 1751.[5] The principal crops there had originally been indigo and rice, while there was some experimentation with silk cultivation.[6] That changed to tobacco, which had become fashionable in Europe and was much in demand. Georgians exported over 6,000,000 pounds of tobacco in 1792, making it the third largest tobacco producer in the new United States.[7] By then the transition to cotton had begun. Under the new code, slaves were allowed religious instruction, but fines were imposed for anyone attempting to teach them to write, and Whites had a standing warrant to search Blacks' homes for weapons. Slaves who re-

---

1 Ibid.
2 Tim McNeese, *American Colonies* (Dayton, OH: Lorenz Educational Press, 2002), 49. See also "As a rule, the sharks followed in the wake of the slave ships." Leif Svalesen, *The Slave Ship Fredensborg*, (Bloomington, IND: Indiana University Press, 2000), 109.
3 "The African Slave Trade," PBS.
4 For more detailed information, see *The Trans-Atlantic Slave Trade Database*, http://www.slavevoyages.org/tast/index.faces.
5 Grant, *The Way It Was in the South*, 53.
6 Joyce E. Chaplin, "Creating a Cotton South in Georgia and South Carolina, 1760-1815," *The Journal of Southern History*, Vol. 57, No. 2, May, 1991, 175.
7 Ibid., 188.

fused to allow searches or who struck a White could be lawfully killed. Owners were initially reimbursed for the value of slaves executed according to court orders.[1]

In 1755 Georgia instituted a pass system that required slaves to have written permission from their owners or overseers to be off the plantation. The new statute also made it legal for owners to maim or emasculate their slaves.[2] Two years later this was reinforced by rural patrols that wandered the countryside and were free to administer up to 20 lashes as punishment of any slave found to be off the owner's property without written permission. In 1770, when Whites began to fear slave uprisings, the legislature forbade groups of seven or more slaves to be on a highway unless accompanied by a White person.[3]

The greatest fear among White Georgians was what they perceived as the vulnerability of their White women. "White Southerners, both inside and outside the legal system, widely shared the belief that black men were obsessed with the desire to rape white women."[4] In rapes of White women by a Negro that came before the judicial system from 1755 to 1865, 100% of the Negro men received the death penalty and were killed.[5] In contrast, "Black on black rape was not thought sufficiently serious to end up in court: the master would handle such cases on the plantation."[6]

The death penalty had been made mandatory for rape or attempted rape of White women by Black men, so the figures are not surprising. Rape of one man's slave by another White man was treated as a trespass against the woman's master, not a crime against the woman.[7] When a master raped one of his own slaves, the law did not hold him accountable.[8] The Georgia code

1 Grant, The Way It Was in the South, 53
2 Peter W. Bardaglio, "Rape and the Law in the Old South: 'Calculated to excite Indignation in every heart,' " The Journal of Southern History, Vol. 60, No. 4, Nov, 1994, 753.
3 Grant, The Way It Was in the South, 54.
4 Bardaglio, "Rape and the Law in the Old South," 752.
5 Glenn McNair, Criminal Injustice: Slaves and Free Blacks in Georgia's Criminal Justice System (Charlottesville, VA: University of Virginia Press, 2009) 154.
6 Grant, The Way It Was in the South, 54.
7 Bardaglio, "Rape and the Law in the Old South," 756.
8 Ibid., 757.

of 1861 asserted rape was "carnal knowledge of a female, whether slave or free, forcibly and against her will."[1] While this was significant progress, a Black man convicted of raping a White woman still received the death penalty, while a White man convicted of raping a slave or free person of color was given a fine and imprisonment at the court's discretion. Lynching slaves suspected of sexual assault against White females was also known in Georgia at the time.[2]

In the "peculiar institution," as Southerners came to call slavery, the experience was not consistent for all. There were cruel masters who brutalized and beat, even killed, their slaves, while there were also kind and generous owners. Though White Southerners would argue that their slaves were happy, the owners lived in constant fear of slave revolts.

Slaves came from many different tribes, and those brought directly from Africa spoke different African languages, so they found it difficult to communicate among themselves, never mind to understand the overseers. This gave rise to the use of pidgin English for communication—and also brutal treatment for failure to follow instructions.

While slaves were considered property, churches saw them as humans with souls that could be saved by God, and many turned to Christianity. As a former slave from South Carolina put it, "If dere ain't a heaven, what's colored folk got to look forward to? They can't get anywhere down here."[3] They might attend a segregated plantation church but combine elements from Africa in their own services held after, and they mixed in song, dance, prayers and eloquent sermons by Black preachers. "It was from their religion, perhaps more than in any other way, that Black slaves who were separated from each other on scattered plantations were able to form a sense of their human unity."[4]

About the time of Catherine's great-grandfather's birth, Georgia had undergone defining changes that were transforming the South and would affect the slaves in residence. With the

---

1 Ibid., 760.
2 Ibid.
3 C. Vann Woodward, "Review: History from Slave Sources," *The American Historical Review*, Vol. 79, No. 2, Apr 1974, 477.
4 Daniel J. Boorstin, and Brooks M. `Kelley, *A History of the United States* (Englewood Cliffs NJ: Prentice Hall, 1989), 229.

birth of industry in England, and machines that could spin and weave fibers, the cultivation of cotton took on new prominence in the lower South, first along the coast and then upcountry. Eli Whitney's invention of the improved cotton gin (for "engine") in 1793 multiplied the ability of workers to separate cotton fiber from seeds. By 1800 the U.S. was producing forty million pounds of cotton annually, which was between 570 and 600 pounds per worker.[1] King Cotton had been given birth. The insatiable demand for cotton products that the British factory system could produce, and British merchant fleet could distribute worldwide, required an expansion of the Southern labor force to provide adequate raw cotton. This was complicated for the Southern states by a Constitutional provision. The international slave trade was only protected by law until 1808.[2] On March 2, 1807, Congress voted to ban importation of slaves into the U.S. as of January 1, 1808,[3] when the Constitutional protection of international slave trade expired. There was a high demand for more slaves, but no legal route for slave importation to increase supply.

The demand for more slave labor motivated a forced breeding campaign by slave owners. In 1830, the price for a prime "field hand" in Georgia was $700. By 1860, the decline in external supply and increased demand had driven it to $1,800.[4] This increase in value had effects on how Georgia slaves were treated when punishment was called for. They had become too valuable to kill or seriously maim, but maintaining discipline while avoiding the feared uprisings remained high concerns. In Georgia this meant more physical mutilation and an increased number of lashes, while the number of executions was reduced as lost slaves could not be replaced. Whether the early Caters were victims of this will never be known, but that state was their home. Again, given the tradition of oral history, the probability is high that Cath-

---

1 Chaplin, "Chaplin, "Creating a Cotton South in Georgia and South Carolina," 194.
2 See *Constitution of the United States*, Art. I, Sec. IX, para. 1.
3 Andrew Glass, "Congress Votes to Ban Slave Trade: March 2, 1807," *Politico*,   http://www.politico.com/story/2009/03/congress-votes-to-ban-slave-trade-march-2-1807-019465, March 2, 2009.
4 Glenn McNair, *Criminal Injustice: Slaves and Free Blacks in Georgia's Criminal Justice System*, (Charlottesville, VA: University of Virginia Press, 2009), 146.

erine heard personal stories and experiences of inhumane treat-ment of Georgia slaves during her formative years.

Most punishment for Blacks was carried out for violations of what was called "plantation law," where the owner or overseer was judge and jury and administered the sentence. Whipping and mutilation were common punishments, though occasion-ally the person charged was killed. Annette Milledge, a former slave recalled the brutality: "Sometimes dey would whoop dem terrible. Dey tied dem acros't a barrel and whoop dem until de blood run out. De leas' little thing dey whoop de hide off 'em."[1]

With fewer executions, physical mutilation took on new sig-nificance in public trials. Branding was used to label the Black person with his crime, such as "M" for murder, "A" for arson, and "B" for burglary. Along with this, the victim's left ear was cropped in the public square. The branding was both to let the public know of their dangerous character and to warn prospec-tive buyers of the threat they posed.[2]

Flogging, or using lashes, became a more prominent punish-ment since the slave would suffer but could still work. The mean number of lashes for Georgia convicts in 1865 was 220, and the median was 195.[3] While this is considerable, the highest level in Georgia was reached in 1856, the year Catherine's grandfather was born, when a man named George was accused of attempting to kill a White man in Emanuel County. George was given a sen-tence of 50 lashes on his bare back each Tuesday for six months, for total of at least 1,200 lashes. Then he was branded with an M and returned to a life of slavery.[4]

Catherine's heritage is part of a shameful episode in Ameri-can history, when equality was eloquently discussed but many White people, who bought and sold their fellow man, and treat-ed them as they would treat animals, did not consider Blacks to be human. How having this in her heritage affected Catherine will remain a mystery. There is no doubt she was well aware of it all and much more. How much of it she knew from her family's own story was never revealed, but it seems unrealistic to think

1 Ibid., 143.
2 Ibid., 147
3 Ibid., 146
4 Ibid., 146.

this did not play a role in her own understanding of who she was and in developing her beliefs in social justice. Her identification with this past was a part of her essence, but it is clear that her overt attitudes changed over time.

CHAPTER 3. CHALLENGES IN THE BAYOUS

Catherine's lineage becomes more specific with her grand-father, Charles C. Cater. He was born in November of 1856 in Georgia.[1] His name first appears in the 1900 census, where he was classified as "Black." This can likely be explained by a change in policy made that year for the classification of individuals by census takers.[2] In every census from the First, in 1790, through the Sixth, in 1840, mixed-race had been never been differentiated from Blacks in the category of race. In 1850, with the Seventh Census, "mulatto" was first added as a category that census takers were to distinguish.[3] Unlike the present day census, racial categories were not self-described but were determined by an enumerator.[4] By the Census of 1890, "Black," "Quadroon," and "Octoroon" were listed along with "mulatto" as separate clas-

1 United States of America, Bureau of the Census. *Twelfth Census of the United States*, 1900 United States Federal Census, the Twelfth Census of the United States, National Archives and Records Administration, Washington, D.C.: Census Place: *Atlanta Ward 4, Fulton, Georgia*; Roll: 199; Page: 2A; Enumeration District: 0063; FHL microfilm: 1240199.
2 On the 1900 Census "Enumerators were to mark "W" for White, "B" for Black, "Ch" for Chinese, "Jp" for Japanese, or "In" for American Indian," *1900 - History - U.S. Census Bureau - Census.gov*, https://www.census.gov/history/www/through_the_decades/index_of_questions/1900_1.html.
3 Christine B. Hickman, "The Devil and the One Drop Rule: Racial Categories, African Americans, and the U.S. Census," *Michigan Law Review*, Vol. 95, No. 5, Mar, 1997, 1184.
4 Ibid., 1185.

sifications, and enumerators were asked to somehow identify each person by visual inspection.[1] But in 1900, the categories of "Quadroon" and "Octoroon" had been eliminated because of difficulties census takers had with making the distinctions, and the Census Bureau found little use for the information.[2] All the individuals on the page for Fulton, Georgia, on which Mr. Cater appears, were categorized as either Black or White,[3] which is because of the limited choices available to census takers that year.[4] That would not be the case in the next census, when Mulatto returned as an option for enumerators.

Racial classification was changed again and by the Fourteenth Census in 1920, Census Bureaus in many places stopped counting "mulattoes" and adopted the "one drop rule" for classifying individuals as Black,[5] so a person with any African heritage detectable to census takers was classified by that heritage. This fit with the changing times and growing influence of eugenics throughout the Progressive Era.

"Mulatto" was the classification that would be used to describe Catherine's grandfather and his children, and eventually Catherine herself. The term "mulatto" was originally an Iberian word, derived from the Latin term for mule, which associated people of mixed blood to mules, the products of mating between a horse and a donkey.[6] In recent decades, references to mixed Black and White heritage have vanished from usage in U.S. terminology, where individuals are categorized as Black or White with no intermediate position.[7] A person like Barack Obama is considered African-American, while in an earlier time he would have been called a mulatto. Such a classification (along with

1 Ibid., 1186.
2 Jennifer Lee and Frank D. Bean, The Diversity Paradox (New York: Russell Sage Foundation, 2010), 39.
3 See Bureau of the Census. Twelfth Census of the United States, 1900.
4 Census enumerators had as choices for "Race or Color": "mark 'W' for White, 'B' for Black, 'Ch' for Chinese, 'Jp' for Japanese, or 'In' for American Indian," "History," United States Census Bureau, https://www.census.gov/history/www/through_the_decades/index_of_questions/1900_1.html
5 Hickman, "The Devil and the One Drop Rule," 1187.
6 Patricia Morton, 'From Invisible Man to "New People': The Recent Discovery of American Mulattoes," Phylon, Vol. 46, No. 2, 2nd Qtr., 1985, 111.
7 Morton, "From Invisible Man to "New People," 107.

many others) exists as a separate group in Latin America and South America and in West Indian societies.[1]

Charles Cater's early years were as a Southerner, and the Civil War began when he was five years old. Although there were some free Blacks, or freedmen, in Georgia prior to the Civil War, they were not welcome by the White population. In October of 1860, five months before the War began, a grand jury called freed Blacks a "nuisance to society" and urged state lawmakers "to pass a law in our next legislature to remove them from our state or sell them into slavery."[2] Some were sold into slavery for incurring small fines or failure to complete official forms. In the Georgia General Assembly, the House of Representatives adopted a bill in November by an 83–48 margin "to allow free persons of color to go into voluntary slavery, or to compel them to move from the state."[3] The session ended before the bill reached the State Senate, and by the time they returned, Lincoln had been inaugurated, leading to the South's secession from the Union.

The bitter Civil War followed, and then Charles was in the post-War Reconstruction South; he was free, as the Thirteenth Amendment to the U.S. Constitution officially ended slavery. The Fourteenth Amendment was adopted when he was 14 years old. When it was passed, *The New York Tribune* reported from Alabama, which would be Catherine's home: "We in Alabama live under a new constitution which secures equal civil rights and political rights to all citizens. The Rebels look sullen, but loyal men breathe freely again—the yoke is lifted off men's necks, and for the first time in these weary years we begin to realize that Slavery is dead."[4] The Fourteenth Amendment made Charles a citizen and guaranteed him due process and equal protection of the laws, but true equality was far from the picture in the South for Black Americans.

Blacks in the South faced challenges in exercising their newly won freedoms, as White supremacy took intimidating forms.

1 Ibid.
2 Clarence L. Mohr, *On The Threshold of Freedom: Masters and Slaves in Civil War Georgia* (Baton Rouge, LA: LSU Press, 2001), 48.
3 Ibid.
4 Special Correspondent, "Complete Restoration of the State – New State Government – Gen. Smith's Inaugural – The United States Senatorship," *New York Tribune*, July 20, 1868, 1.

Among the most dangerous was the Ku Klux Klan that was founded after the War and that, for a time, resorted to lynching and other means of terrorizing those who imposed Reconstruction on the defeated South. They resisted Republican-controlled "Reconstructionist" White Northern leaders and their Southern sympathizers, as well as any Blacks who sought to be involved in politics. Charles' father, Jack Tate, may have been tempting fate as he registered to vote in Alabama as a "colored" native person in 1867.[1]

Ulysses S. Grant, the commanding Union general who was elected president as a Republican in 1868, said the Klan was determined, "by force and terror, to prevent all political action not in accord with the views of the members, to deprive colored citizens of the right to bear arms and of the right of a free ballot, to suppress the schools in which colored children were taught, and to reduce the colored people to a condition closely allied to that of slavery."[2] Congress passed laws and there were court cases aimed at reducing Klan terrorism, but White supremacy had been reestablished in the South. Through intimidation, Democrats took control of all Southern state legislatures in the 1870s, and the Klan went into a period of decline, but it was revived by White Protestant nativist groups as the new century arrived.[3]

The prevailing theories of human origin were long used to justify oppression of Blacks during Reconstruction and the slavery preceding that period. One Southern view that was used to validate the belief that Blacks were an inferior species was that they had descended from a separate Adam, outside the Garden of Eden, and were not truly a part of the human family.[4] That made ownership of them the same as ownership of livestock, and sex with them was similar to bestiality. It was contended

---

1 Alabama 1867 Voter Registration Records Database. Alabama Department of Archives and History, Montgomery, Alabama.
2 Quoted in James Michael Martinez, *Carpetbaggers, Cavalry, and the Ku Klux Klan: Exposing the Invisible Empire During Reconstruction* (Lanham, MD: Rowman & Littlefield, 2007), 24.
3 "Ku Klux Klan - Facts & Summary - HISTORY.com," http://www.history.com/topics/ku-klux-klan.
4 Mason Stokes, "Someone's in the Garden with Eve: Race, Religion, and the American Fall," *American Quarterly*, Vol. 50, No. 4, Dec 1998, 718.

that the offspring of these different species, Whites and Blacks, would be sterile, like mules,[1] or, as the offspring of such relationships were called, mulattoes.

Many adopted a view that had been around for centuries; they were called "Pre-Adamites." They asserted that certain races, including the Blacks, were not descended from Adam and Eve at all, but that God had created them on an earlier day in creation. This solved the problem of Cain's wife[2] and allowed for White supremacy to be seen as having religious sanction. Soon after the Civil War, Buckner H. Payne (a clergyman and publisher from Nashville, Tennessee), was writing under the pseudonym Ariel.[3] Payne assured his readers that Noah and his sons who survived the great flood had been white and had, long straight hair, high noses and thin lips. He stated, "The Negro is a separate and distinct species of the genus homo from Adam and Eve and being distinct from them, that it unquestionably follows that the Negro was created before Adam and Eve."[4] God had decided to destroy the world, according to Payne, as punishment for miscegenation, the racial mixing of Whites and soulless Blacks.[5] The racially pure clan of Noah survived this justified action of total genocide by flood, as did the Blacks, though "the Negro entered the ark only as a beast."[6] His short book ignited a firestorm of pamphlets and considerable controversy in the South following its 1867 release, with both supporters of Payne's thesis and many unfavorable tracts published by religious leaders. However, all of them supported

1 Keith Sealing, "Blood Will Tell: Scientific Racism and the Legal Prohibition Against Miscegenation," SSRN 1260015, 2000 - papers. ssrn.com, 2000, 562.
2 In Genesis 4 the first two people, Adam and Eve, have two sons, Cain and Abel. Cain killed his brother Abel. God put a mark on Cain's face and he was exiled to the land of Nod, east of Eden. There he and his wife conceived the child Enoch. The question has been, where did Cain's wife come from when she arrived in Nod? If there had been a separate creation before Adam and Eve, she could have descended from an earlier "Adam."
3 Buckner H. 'Ariel' Payne, *The Negro: What Is His Ethnological Status* (Cincinnati: self published, 1867).
4 Ibid., 22.
5 Colin Kidd, *The Forging of Races: Race and Scripture in the Protestant Atlantic World, 1600–2000* (Cambridge, UK: Cambridge University Press, 2006), 150-151.
6 "Ariel" (Buckner H. Payne), *The Negro*, 20.

White supremacy as Biblically ordained, for different reasons.[1]

Those who believed man descended from more than a unique first couple were known in general as polygenists, and as the nineteenth century came to an end, there was more popular literature to reinforce their beliefs. A. Hoyle Lester's *The Pre-Adamite, or Who Tempted Eve*,[2] told of a bored and unfulfilled Eve who roamed from the Garden, where she met a stranger and was seduced, then gave birth to the "mongrel offspring," Cain, the ancestor of the "negro race."[3] More extreme was Charles Carroll, who wrote *The Negro a Beast*[4] in 1900, and a Pre-Adamite tale, *The Tempter of Eve*,[5] two years later. The tempter was a Negro maid who had served Eve and at times had given her advice. Carroll wrote that it was Adam and Eve's duty "to control it [their maid] in common with the rest of the animals," but instead they had accepted the maid as a social equal. This was the true original sin. In Carroll's words: "It was man's social equality with the negro that brought sin into the world."[6,7]

While the South endured Reconstruction and its difficult world for the non-Whites, Charles Cater remained in Georgia. There, he met Jack Tate and Jennie's daughter Mary, who was born in Alabama in August of 1864. On December 19, 1884, in Fulton County, Georgia, the two were married. He was 28 years old at the time and she was 20. By this time Jim Crow laws were disenfranchising Blacks in the South and further enforcing second-class citizenship and degradation.

Two cases came before the Supreme Court, one an antecedent for the other, and made segregation the official law of the

1 See Forrest G. Wood, *Black Scare: The Racist Response to Emancipation and Reconstruction* (Berkeley: University of California Press, 1968) 6-8.
2 A Hoyle Lester, *The Pre-Adamite, or Who Tempted Eve* (Philadelphia: J.B. Lippincott, 1875).
3 Stokes, "Someone's in the Garden with Eve, 724.
4 Charles Carroll, *The Negro a Beast* (St. Louis: American Book and Bible House, 1900).
5 Charles Carroll, *The Tempter of Eve* (St. Louis: Adamic Publishing Co., 1902).
6 Quotes from pages 402-406 of Carroll, *The Tempter of Eve*, appearing in Mason Stokes, *The Color of Sex: Whiteness, Heterosexuality, and the Fictions of White Supremacy* (Durham, N.C, Duke University Press, 2001), 97-98.
7 On differences in southern theories of human origin in the late nineteenth century, including mongenism, polygenism, see Robert Dodge, *Andrea and Sylvester* (New York: Algora Publishing, 2015) 25- 26.

land. Now, life in the Jim Crow South was an even greater challenge for Blacks. The first case, *Pace v. Alabama*, ended in 1883.[1] That case involved the Alabama Criminal Code which made adultery and fornication between unmarried partners a crime. The punishment, if the partners were of the same race, was a fine of not less than $100 and could include jail time of up to six months. If the partners were a White person and a Negro, who intermarried, lived in adultery or fornication, the punishment was hard labor for two to seven years.[2] The Supreme Court ruled that this disparity was not a violation of civil rights and the "equal protection of the laws" provision of the Fourteenth Amendment, since the punishment was the same for each offending person, whether White or Black.[3]

This "separate but equal" decision was a significant antecedent to the Court's 1896 ruling involving segregated trains. That case, *Plessy v. Ferguson*,[4] made "separate but equal" the law of the land. That decision would be of lasting importance in alienating and marginalizing Blacks by legalizing segregation in all situations and facilities, where separate rarely meant equal.[5] Segregation was extended nationally and the Jim Crow South was in full flower.

It was in this situation that Charles and Mary Cater began a family. While being Black and in the South would make life a challenge and a constant affront to personal dignity, there are indications that in some ways they may not have suffered as much as others. How this distinction influenced the Cater family and was passed on to Catherine is unknown, but it might have played a part in her later seemingly inconsistent attitude about outwardly protesting racial injustice.

The Caters, Mary and Charles, were not a typical Black couple and might be better considered as being among the prominent members of Atlanta's racial minority of their time. Charles

1 *Pace v Alabama*, 106 US 583, 584, 1882.
2 *U.S. Supreme Court, Pace v. Alabama, 106 U.S. 583* (1883) https://supreme.justia.com/cases/federal/us/106/583/
3 *Pace v. Alabama*, 106.
4 *Plessy v. Ferguson*, 163 US 537, 1896.
5 Werner Sollors, *Interracialism: Black-white Intermarriage in American History, Literature, and Law* ☐ (New York: Oxford University Press, 2000), 65.

had been a teacher and an entrepreneur, and he became a gro-cer.[1] A study of the Negro bourgeoisie in Atlanta from 1890–1910 found the several grocers to be included in the leading figures in the Black community. They served a primarily Negro clientele and were part of the elite class that mostly came from mulatto, house-servant backgrounds.[2] They had advantages compared to field hands that included being able to elevate their status and economic standing, and sometimes they maintained close rela-tionships with Whites.[3] In summarizing the members who con-stituted this group, it was reported, "Life for the mulatto aristoc-racy of old Atlanta (circa 1890–1910) centered primarily around the respectable First Congregational Church, select Atlanta University and perhaps a dozen exclusive social clubs. Many of the elite themselves had been educated at Congregational-ist Atlanta University (or its affiliated grammar and secondary school) and ordinarily sent their children there to be prepared for teaching and other white collar occupations."[4] Mary Cater was a graduate of Atlanta University in the class of 1880.[5] At-lanta University, sometimes referred to as Atlanta College, was founded in 1865 by the American Missionary Association and was the first graduate institution in the nation formed to serve an African-American student body.[6]

Charles and Mary began their family when he was 29. Their firstborn was Charles Jr., in Atlanta on July 26, 1886. Three years later, on August 2, 1889, Mary had a second son, James Tate, also born in Atlanta. James would eventually be Catherine's father. The next year Mary gave birth to a girl, Hattie, in November. Charles was 38 and Mary 30 when their third son, Douglas, ar-

1 Occupation on Bureau of the Census. *Twelfth Census of the United States*, Atlanta Ward 4, 1900.
2 August Meier and David Lewis, "History of the Negro Upper Class in Atlanta, Georgia, 1890-1958," *The Journal of Negro Education*, Vol. 28, No. 2, Spring 1959, 130.
3 Ibid.
4 Ibid., 130-131.
5 *Catalogue of the Officers and Students of Atlanta University, 1909-1910* (Atlanta: Atlanta University Press, Book 41, 1910), 40.
6 "About CAU: History," http://www.cau.edu/about/cau-history. html, Clark University was founded in 1969, four years after Atlanta University. The two consolidated in 1988 to form Clark Atlanta University.

rived in April of 1895. A year later it was boy number four, as Roscoe was born on October 27, 1896.

On the 1900 census report, Hattie is listed as a schoolgirl and James as a schoolboy.[1] Included in the household was a sister-in-law, twenty-four-year-old Eunice Simpson, a single teacher, who like all others had her race listed as Black. The final listing in the Cater household, who no doubt lightened Mary's burden, was a nineteen-year-old married woman, Georgia Green. She was no relation to the others, but was listed as the cook.[2] Mary's burden was greater than a cook could relieve, as for unknown reasons she died in 1906 at the age of 42. In 1908 Charles remarried, and his second wife, Clara, was also an alumnus of Atlanta College, having graduated in 1886.[3]

All of Charles and Mary's five children went on to attend Atlanta University, which was a formidable achievement. While James would be the great influence on Catherine, circumstances would lead her to spend time with several of the members of this family in her formative years. The Atlanta University they attended was for African-Americans, and it included a high school as a preparatory school. Its entrance requirements were traditional and demanding. It is safe to say that few in the contemporary world could have met the standards. College entrance requirements during the time Charles' children attended included Greek, Latin, biology, physics, mathematics (arithmetic, algebra, geometry), English (composition, literature, the Bible), history (Hebrew, Greek, Roman, French, English, U.S.), as well as industrial training for boys and sewing and dressmaking for girls.[4] Once admitted, tuition was $2 per course per month, while board with furnished room was $10 per month in the first years, then rose to $11. All students were required to work at least an hour per day, and if boarding, their labors would lower their expenses.[5]

The university curriculum for all students was as follows: freshman studied Greek, Algebra and Geometry in the first se-

1 Bureau of the Census. *Twelfth Census of the United States*, Atlanta Ward 4, 1900.
2 Ibid.
3 *Catalogue of the Officers and Students of Atlanta University, 1909-1910*, 40.
4 Ibid., 9.
5 Ibid., 20

mester, then Latin, Literature and Elocution in the second. In the sophomore year it was a semester of Greek and German, followed by a semester of Latin, Geometry, and Trigonometry. Junior year brought Argumentation, Bible, Elocution, Civics, and Economics first, followed by a semester of Chemistry, Geology, and History. In the senior year they studied Sociology, Physics, and Astronomy, and for their final semester it was Psychology, Ethics, and French or Pedagogy.[1] Accompanying this was the required work and some education in manual labor.

By the census of 1910, the number of Charles Cater's household had grown to ten. His new wife of two years by that time, the 44-year-old Clara, had three children of her own. Charles' occupation was described as "proprietor of Grocery Store,"[2] which may or may not have represented a change from its previous description as a "grocer." Still in his household were his children by Mary, 23-year-old Charles Jr., James T., age 20, Douglas, who was 15, Hattie, 14, and Roscoe 19. How Hattie became younger than Douglas and Roscoe during the ten years between censuses can only be accounted for by an error in the taking or reporting. Clara's children went by the last name Maxwell, and her oldest, Louise, was James' age. She was in education, a public school teacher. Next was Clara's daughter May, 15, then her son, Leigh, 13. The two females were listed as Charles Cater's step-daughters and Leigh was listed as his stepson.[3] Like all the Caters, Clara and her children were classified as mulattoes.[4]

1 Ibid., 7.
2 Bureau of the Census. *Thirteenth Census of the United States,* Atlanta Ward 4, 1910.
3 Ibid.
4 Ibid.

CHAPTER 4. THE COCOON IN JIM CROW ALABAMA

James Tate Cater had graduated from Atlanta University in 1909 "With Highest Honor,"[1] the only member of his class to achieve such a high distinction. The following fall he was employed as a teacher at that institution,[2] and the census of 1910 listed the 20-year-old as a college teacher in Georgia.[3]

His considerable education in classical thought and languages was to be shared with his daughter, Catherine, from when she was at an early age.

James' career as a teacher at his alma mater, Atlanta University, was not a long one. He had begun there in the fall of 1909, but their catalogue of the 1911–1912 school year listed him as a student at Harvard,[4] so he taught at Atlanta for at most two years. By the time of his move to Harvard, he was drawing attention from leading members in the African-American community.

---

1 *Catalogue of the Officers and Students of Atlanta University, 1909-1910*, 18, 22.
2 Ibid., 37.
3 Bureau of the Census, *Thirteenth Census of the United States*, Atlanta Ward 4, 1910.
4 *The Atlanta University Bulletin:* The Catalogue 1911-1912, Atlanta: Atlanta University, *Atlanta University Catalogs.* Book 42. s. II no. 7, April 1912, 38. Available online at http://digitalcommons.auctr.edu/aucatalogs/42.

Among those who had taken note of James was his former instructor, W. E. Du Bois.[1] Du Bois was the first African-American
to receive a PhD from Harvard,[2] and he was one of the cofound-
ers of the National Association for the Advancement of Colored
People, the NAACP.[3] He established and edited a magazine, *The
Crisis*, which was the official publication of the NAACP. In the
February 1912 issue of the magazine there was a story with the
title "Along the Color Line" that reported, "James Tate Cater, a
graduate of Atlanta University, '09, and at present a senior at
Harvard College, is assistant in mathematics at this the oldest
university in America."[4]

The following fall James took a new position on the faculty
of Straight University in New Orleans, Louisiana. The university
had been originally established by the American Missionary Association of the Congregational Church and was built with assistance from the Freedman's Bureau, primarily to serve recently
freed slaves who mainly had very little or no education. While
it served the African-American community, the university grew
and added professional schools, and the student body included some White students as well. The university's mission was
spelled out in an 1878 American Missionary Association article,
which stated:

> The Results We Hope To Accomplish.
>
> In a word, our aim is Education, in its broadest and
> best meaning. The elevation, the prosperity, the highest
> manhood, and the co-ordinate rank of the African race
> in America, in the friendly rivalry of races . . . That the
> race is not educated, is by no fault of theirs. That they
> desire education is to their credit. To help them to this
> education is both our duty and our privilege.[5]

1 *Finding Aid to the Catherine Cater Papers*: Biography, 2. Catherine Cater
Collection, North Dakota State University Institute for Regional
Studies & Universities Archives, Fargo, ND.
2 Thomas D. Boston, "W. E. B. Du Bois and the Historical School of
Economics," *The American Economic Review*, Vol. 81, No. 2, May 1991, 304.
3 See Laura B. Randolph, *Ebony*, "The NAACP Turns 80," Vol. 44, No. 9,
July 1989 126, 128, 130.
4 "Along the Color Line," *The Crisis*, Vol. 3, No. 4, Feb 1912, 140.
5 Rev. W. S. Alexander, "The Freedmen: Straight University: New

By the time James came to New Orleans in 1912, this remained the goal. When he was there he met Daisy Ronchon, from French-speaking St. Martinville, Louisiana,[1] the daughter of Victor Ronchon and Catherine McCoy.[2] Before meeting James, Daisy had been a servant in the Brandon household in New Orleans.[3] James continued to gain renown in the Black community as an educator, and his biography was included in the 1915 edition of *Who's Who of the Colored Race*.[4]

In the summer of 1915 James was registered in graduate school in mathematics at the University of Chicago.[5] It was his introduction to an institution that would have considerable influence on him that he would share with Catherine in time.

On June 3, 1916, Daisy and James, both 26, were married.[6] A family soon followed as Daisy gave birth to a daughter on March 18, 1917.[7] They named their daughter Althea, after an aunt, with the middle name Catherine. Catherine explained many years later that she never went by the name Althea, which was pronounced "Al-tay" by the French speakers. In her words, "I've never used it. Most people have a difficult time wrapping their tongues around it."[8] She would be Catherine for her entire life.

Orleans, Louisiana," *American Missionary* Volume 32, Issue 6, June 1878, 172.

1 Box 1, file 2, Catherine Cater Collection, North Dakota State University (NDSU) Institute for Regional Studies & Universities Archives, Fargo, ND.

2 "Georgia Deaths, 1914–1927" and "Georgia Deaths, 1930," images, FamilySearch, Georgia Department of Health and Vital Statistics, Atlanta, Georgia.

3 Bureau of the Census. *Thirteenth Census of the United States, New Orleans Ward 14, Orleans, Louisiana*; Roll: T624_524; Page: 11B; Enumeration District: 0224; FHL microfilm: 1374537.

4 *Who's Who Of The Colored Race V1, 1915: A General Biographical Dictionary Of Men And Women Of African Descent, Volume One* (Fort Wayne, IN, U.S.A: Hyde Brothers, Booksellers, 1915) 61.

5 *The Annual Register of the University of Chicago, 1915-1916* (Chicago: The University of Chicago Press, Sept 1916) 446.

6 Secretary of State, State of Louisiana, *Vital Records Indices*, Division of Archives, Records Management, and History, Baton Rouge, LA.

7 Records of the U.S. Customs Service, Record Group 36, National Archives at Washington, D.C. *Passenger and Crew Lists of Vessels Arriving at New York, New York, 1897-1957*, Passenger list, US Citizens aboard the *Gripsholm* sailing from Gothenburg Sweden, arriving in New York on August 24, 1946.

8 Nancy Edmonds Hanson, "Catherine Cater: Her Former Students at Moorhead State and NDSU Repeatedly Describe Her as 'A Great Teacher'," *Howard Binford's Guide to Fargo, Moorhead, and West Fargo*, Vol. 15, No. 3, Sept 1983, 20. Box 1, File 19, Catherine Cater Collection, North Dakota State University Archives, Fargo, ND.

Catherine Cater was born just over two weeks before the U.S. entered the Great War, later known as World War I. As her parents celebrated the arrival of their daughter and the beginning of a family, the outside world threatened to intrude in their lives. James was called to register for the draft, as America had entered the war after Germany had begun unrestricted submarine warfare and was sinking American ships. President Woodrow Wilson, who had been reelected in 1916 on the slogan "He kept us out of war," asked for a declaration of war on April 2 that was approved by Congress two days later. On June 5, James was in New Orleans registering for conscription. His Draft Registration Card had the 27-year-old teacher listed as employed by the American Mission School and living at 2346 Canal Street in New Orleans. After first writing "African," he had crossed that out and listed his race as "Negro," and described himself as being "slender" and standing five feet, four inches tall, having grey eyes and brown hair, but bald.[1] Catherine's birth was timely, as James was able to apply for an exemption from the draft on the basis of being sole support for his wife and child.[2] Catherine inherited her father's small-statured physical characteristics.

He wasn't called up, though his older brother was,[3] and a new job beckoned. James was offered the position of Dean of Talladega College, in Talladega, Alabama, a position second in authority only to the school's president. In 1918 it would become his longtime academic home. Talladega College had begun on November 20, 1865, when two former slaves met with a group

---

1 United States, Selective Service System, *World War I Selective Service System Draft Registration Cards, 1917-1918*, Louisiana; Registration County: Orleans; Roll: 1684818; Draft Board: 02, National Archives and Records Administration, Washington, D.C.
2 Ibid.
3 Charles Jr. was 28 and described as "short" with a "medium" build on his draft card. United States, Selective Service System. *World War I Selective Service System Draft Registration Cards, 1917-1918. Georgia;* Registration County: *Fulton;* Roll: *1556947;* Draft Board: *4,* National Archives and Records Administration. M1509, 4,582 rolls, Washington, D.C. On the census of 1930 he is listed as a veteran of the World War. *Fifteenth Census of the United States, 1930.* Washington, D.C.: National Archives and Records Administration, 1930. T626, 2,667 rolls, *Atlanta, Fulton, Georgia;* Roll: *361;* Page: *22B;* Enumeration District: *0059;* Image: *672.0;* FHL microfilm: *2340096.*

of freedmen in Mobile, Alabama, and persuaded them to commit to providing a school for the children of former slaves. Originally a one-room schoolhouse built from used lumber, the Freedmen Bureau persuaded the American Missionary Association to purchase the Baptist Academy that had defaulted on its mortgage and was available. The building was an example of inspirational Southern architecture, a massive three-story structure fronted by giant Doric columns supporting a typical Greek temple pediment. It had originally been built by slave labor to house White students, but in 1867 it opened as Alabama's first private liberal arts college dedicated to educating African-Americans.[1] While designed for African-Americans, Talladega came to attract a White population as well, notably in its law school and other professional schools. Catherine recalled that it was "Integrated in a segregated town of the same name and students were admitted on the basis of demonstrated capacities, rather than background knowledge."[2]

In the 1920 Census, both Daisy and James as well as Catherine, aged two years, 10 months, were listed as "Mulatto" under the category of "race."[3] Tragedy soon struck the family. On March 24, 1921, for reasons unknown, 31-year-old Daisy died.[4] Daisy was laid to rest in the Oakland Cemetery of Atlanta[5] with James' parents, Charles and Mary. Catherine had turned four only five days earlier and she was now without a mother. The home environment created for her by her father in the years that followed did much to mold the Catherine many us would come to know in a much different time and place.

Catherine attended elementary school in Talladega. She grew, isolated to a degree from the subjugation of Blacks in Alabama in the 1920s, and surrounded by classical education and

1 "Talladega College History," http://www.talladega.edu/history.asp.
2 Hanson, "Catherine Cater," 20.
3 Department of Commerce, Bureau of the Census, *Fourteenth Census of the United States*, 1920 United States Federal Census, National Archives and Records Administration, Talladega Ward 2, Talladega, Alabama; Roll: T625_41; Page: 6A; Enumeration District: 136; Image: 796.
4 State of Georgia, *Indexes of Vital Records for Georgia: Deaths, 1919-1998*. Georgia, USA: Georgia Health Department, Office of Vital Records, 1998.
5 "Find a Grave: Daisy Cater," http://www.findagrave.com/cgibin/fg.cg i?page=gsr&GSln=Cater&GSiman=1&GScid=35955&.

scholarship on a personal level from an early age. This was a true Southern town that had a "Faulknerian courthouse square which witnesse[d] the regular passage of wagons loaded with cotton bales."[1] Her family home was in the foothills of the Blue Ridge Mountains and included a large library. Their pet schnauzer, Otto, could keep her company in the garden or on walks, but it was her father who was her main companion.

There were difficult times in her early years that would stay with her. Her recollection as recounted is difficult to unravel, since Nancy Hanson reported her as saying that as a young girl Catherine loved parades and was drawn to the sound of one. It was the Ku Klux Klan marching in Talladega near the college, and her "family" rushed her inside to hide her under her bed.[2] This implies that both her father and mother were involved, so the event took place when Catherine was at most four years old. She next says that Catherine learned the following morning that the father of one of her playmates had been hanged,[3] and then quotes Catherine: "We simply didn't go into the town. But my father was very concerned that we have all the opportunities other children had."[4] The final sentence seems to indicate her mother was not in the picture at the time. In any event, it was a memorable experience for the young child and there would be other similar encounters, as feelings and attitudes were being etched in Catherine's mind.

Years later, she was asked about the impact on her from growing up in the South, with a cotton mill not far away and Ku Klux Klan members, the night raiders, wandering through the streets. "These things affect you," Catherine said quietly, reported NDSU *Spectrum* reporter Ellen Kosse.[5]

---

1 Paul Homan, "A Humanist in Honors: Another Look at Catherine Cater," *Journal of the National Collegiate Honors Council* - Online Archive, Paper 193, http://digitalcommons.unl.edu/nchcjournal/193, Fall/Winter, 2000, 87.
2 Hanson, "Catherine Cater," 21.
3 Ibid.
4 Ibid.
5 Ellen Kosse, "Cater: 'infect one another with the desire to learn,' " *Spectrum* (North Dakota State University), Feb 8, 1977, 6. Box 1, Folder 17, Catherine Cater Collection, North Dakota State University Archives, Fargo, ND.

Catherine completed elementary school in Talladega, then was passed on to relatives mainly in the North for her junior high school years. Her interviews do not explain why this was the case, whether it was to broaden Catherine's experiences or to give her father a break from raising a young child while holding a demanding work position. Likely both were factors, and it also gave James more freedom, perhaps, to more openly pursue a new relationship since he was single again. While Catherine did not refer to this in interviews recalling her early years, there is evidence indicating that her father's life may have changed while Catherine was having her first experience in the North.

Catherine's junior high school experience included living with relatives in Chicago and New York, and may have included a stay in Charleston.[1] Catherine indicated that she lived with her Aunt Hattie,[2] and she may have spent much of the time in her junior high school years with Hattie, given the occupations and locations of her father's siblings. After graduating from Atlanta University, Hattie had gone on to Fisk,[3] an exclusive school for African-Americans, and following that she became a teacher at the Bryant Prep School in Atlanta.[4] She then made a career change, and by the 1920 census was working for the Associated Press.[5] During the 1920 census she was listed as a "district visitor" in Georgia at age 28, and she later lived in New York City. Hattie's Associated Press work, while she was hosting Catherine, is likely the reason for Catherine's reason for visits to the large cities of the North.

1 Hannah Vanorny, interview of Catherine Cater, April 13, 2005, Box 1, File 7, Tape B, Catherine Cater Collection, North Dakota State University Archives, Fargo, ND. This interview is the single mention of Charleston.

2 Ibid.

3 *The Catalogue 1912–1913* (Atlanta: Atlanta University) The Atlanta University Bulletin, Atlanta University Catalogs, series II no. 11, Book 43, 1913, 38.

4 *The Catalogue 1915-1916* (Atlanta: Atlanta University) Atlanta University Catalogs.54, The Atlanta University Bulletin, series II, no. 23, April 1916, 54.

5 *Fourteenth Census of the United States, 1920*, National Archives, Washington, D.C. NARA microfilm publication T625, 2076 rolls, Records of the Bureau of the Census, Record Group 29. Atlanta Ward 4, Fulton, Georgia; Roll: T625_250; Page: 19A; Enumeration District: 87; Image: 802.

Her visit to Charleston could have been hosted by one of James' other siblings, who appear to have been tied closely to Georgia during the 1920s, but whose work might have taken them elsewhere. Charles Jr. was a medical doctor,[1] while his younger brother Roscoe was the president of a haberdashery, and the baby of the family, Roscoe, was a cashier for an insurance company.[2]

Catherine recalled school in Chicago as very different from in the South. She didn't stand with the other students at the first school assembly, since she was not aware of what was happening. Following the event, she was called out and made to memorize the Gettysburg Address. For not standing at the opening assembly, at the next school assembly she had to get up in front of the entire school and recite Lincoln's words.[3] This was an unforgettably frightening experience for a young female about to enter her teens and still new to the school.

She was put in the lowest academic level of the sections of the 8th grade classes and found that textbooks in Chicago had a very different view of the Civil War from that in the South, including who won.[4]

Catherine recalled being at her aunt's in New York (Hattie was her only aunt) where she saw a Ku Klux Klan march.[5] This memory raises a question of timing for Catherine's whereabouts, since the 1920s Klan rise peaked in 1925 in its spread to northern cities,[6] and Catherine was in grade eight in Chicago, making it likely the late 1920s, then New York followed. Perhaps her New York stay preceded her Chicago visit, but junior high began in grade seven. So she may have been moving back and forth between cities in the late twenties when she was with Hattie. Catherine was unclear on her early years, and said, "It was a rambling sort of life. I never had much of a sense of roots."[7] What seems likely about her Ku Klux Klan observation and New York City is that she encountered a demonstration over Al Smith, the

1 *The Catalogue 1912–1913*, Atlanta, 38.
2 *Fourteenth Census of the United States, 1920*, Atlanta Ward 4.
3 Vanorny, interview of Catherine Cater, Tape A.
4 Ibid.
5 Ibid.
6 Boorstin, and `Kelley, *A History of the United States*, 484.
7 Hanson, "Catherine Cater" 20.

New York governor who captured the 1928 Democratic Party nomination for the presidency of the United States. Smith was the first Catholic ever to be nominated for the presidency. A revived Ku Klux Klan in New York and across the country "became actively involved in preventing a Catholic from ever getting near the White House, going all out to defeat Smith. One Klan leader mailed thousands of postcards after Democrats nominated the New Yorker, stating firmly, 'We now face the darkest hour in American history. In a convention ruled by political Romanism, anti-Christ has won.' "[1]

Catherine returned to Talladega and would remain in Alabama for high school, then attend college in the school where her father was dean. During these years he treated her as an adult and they had lengthy conversations, "marvelous conversations."[2] Though his advanced training was in mathematics, he had a broad background in humanities, including languages. She recalls, "I can still see him walking down the stairs on mornings when he felt especially fine, quoting from Milton's *Paradise Lost*. It was a nice growing up."[3] Her father was especially interested in the approach Robert Hutchins was taking to education at the University of Chicago, and he passed his enthusiasm along to his daughter.[4]

Robert Hutchins had come from being Dean of Yale Law School to the University of Chicago as its 30-year-old president in 1929. The university that he inherited was a very John Dewey pragmatism-oriented institution. Hutchins co-taught a Great Books seminar with philosopher Mortimer Adler and became especially fascinated with Plato and Aquinas. Under Adler's influence, he developed a new curriculum that would have impact nationwide, built on studying Great Books and giving comprehensive exams.[5] About the basis of his new curriculum, he said:

---

1 Robert A. Slayton, "When a Catholic Terrified the Heartland," *New York Times*, Oct 10, 2011.
2 Vanorny, interview of Catherine Cater, Tape A.
3 Hanson, "Catherine Cater" 21.
4 Vanorny, interview of Catherine Cater, Tape A.
5 For a comprehensive discussion, see George W. Dell, "Robert M. Hutchins' Philosophy of General Education and the College at the University of Chicago." *The Journal of General Education,* Vol. 30, No.1, Spring 1978.

"What are the permanent studies? They are in the first place those books which have through the centuries attained the dimensions of classics . . . A classic is a book that is contemporary in every age. That is why it is a classic. The conversations of Socrates raise questions that are as urgent today as they were when Plato wrote . . . Such books are then a part, and a large part, of the permanent studies . . . How can we call a man educated who has not read any of the great books in the western world? . . . It was the colossal triumph of the Greeks and Romans and of the great thinkers of the Middle Ages to sound the depths of almost every problem which human nature has to offer, and to interpret human thought and human aspiration with astounding profundity and insight."[1]

This man and his ideas were there subject of conversation between Catherine and her father, and they discussed his views, the great books and the ideas presented as they related to the modern world. The influence on Catherine is evident. Her father attempted to implement some of Hutchins' ideas at Talladega. His belief in the value of exposure to the great books became a requirement of two years of immersion, studying the greatest and most historically influential works written in the social, physical, biological sciences and the humanities first, before students went into majors.

Following high school Catherine remained in Talladega for college, beginning in the middle of the Depression, 1934. Catherine's studies included the Hutchins system her father had added, recalling, "I had the benefit of their experience myself, and so I'm deeply indebted to the system."[2]

While the education was good and she had her comfortable home, it was still Alabama. She was reminded of the dangers surrounding her on a day when she went out bicycle riding in the woods with a German–Dutch friend from school; they came upon a man who had been hanged and was dangling from a tree.[3] While I was in college, I recall listening to her tell me of witnessing Klan hangings when she was young, but the conversa-

1 Robert Maynard Hutchins, *The Higher Learning in America*, (New Haven: Yale University Press, 1936) 78—80.
2 Hanson, "Catherine Cater," 21.
3 Vanorny, interview of Catherine Cater, Tape A.

tion never went beyond that point. In an interview she spoke of the Klan including bankers and lawyers, and she added that lynchings did not appear in the newspaper. The Klan marched through the Talladega campus on another occasion which was in Catherine's final years or shortly after she left but while her father remained in charge.

By the time she was a senior, Catherine was a bespectacled young woman with very short-cropped hair and a trim physique like her father's. She had plenty to keep herself busy, as along with her studies, she was president of the Talladega College student branch of the NAACP.[1] Though she was an African-American, a Negro by Alabama law, her photograph from the time shows a young woman with dark hair and dark eyes but skin that appears rather light.[2] She was also editor of a new campus publication, "The Sandalwood."[3] Catherine, described as having been "a brilliant student,"[4] majored in English literature while philosophy was her minor. When she graduated in the spring, she had begun to master the areas that she would develop for another 77 years.

The outside pressures and persecution as well as the intellectual stimulation molded the young woman, as she reported in interviews. During her years away, another story developed that might have played a part as well, though interviewers did not raise this question with Catherine. Her father, James, had been doing more than acting as dean while Catherine was growing up in Talladega. It appears that it is not possible to track down the beginning of the story, or to know how it overlaps with Catherine's relationship with her father and the time he spent with her.

Catherine left Alabama in the fall of 1938 to continue her education at the University of Michigan. Perhaps things happened quickly after she left, or things could have been going on since she was in the North with Hattie as a young girl. In the 1940 census, the report on Catherine's father, James, revealed new

1 "College Ed.," *Pittsburgh Courier*, May 28, 1938, 2.
2 Ibid.
3 Ibid.
4 "Dr. Cornelius Golightly (1917-1976): The Life of an Academic and Public Intellectual," *BlackPast.org*, http://www.blackpast.org/perspectives/dr-cornelius-golightly-1917-1976-life-academic-and-public-intellectual.

information. She was no longer in his household, but he was the head of a family. He was still listed as Dean of Talladega, but with a 40-year-old wife, Ermine L. Cater, a Negro who was born in Georgia. They had two children, James T., age 13, born in Alabama, and Sidney, age 5, born in Illinois.[1] Catherine had a stepmother and two half-brothers that had become a part of her life and she would have to share her father's affections. Whether James and Ermine produced the children is uncertain, but the name James for the older one, and their birthplaces (Alabama, where Catherine's father lived, and Illinois, where he attended graduate school and likely visited to see Hutchins' program in action, and for conferences as an administrator and a member of the American Mathematical Association), may be indicative.

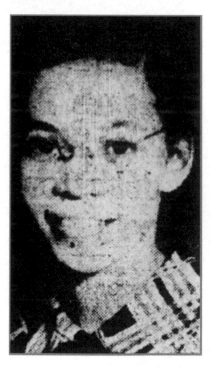

Catherine as a senior in college, 1938

The Pittsburgh Courier

---

1 *Sixteenth Census of the United States, 1940.* Washington, D.C.: National Archives and Records Administration, 1940. T627, 4,643 rolls, *Talladega, Talladega, Alabama;* Roll: *T627_81;* Page: *22A;* Enumeration District: *61-14.*

Catherine was leaving her father and trusted companion behind, along with the intellectual discussions they enjoyed. Would he carry that on with Ermine, whose education ended at grade four?[1] The question of when their relationship began is compounded by the fact that neither James nor Ermine appears on the 1930 census, nor was their marriage recorded in any accessible record.

Regardless of the uncertainty of this relationship, which she kept private through her later years, and how it all affected Catherine's mindset, she had received a fine education. Her father had contributed much to preparing her to head north to begin her graduate work.

---

1 Ibid.

CHAPTER 5. HEADING NORTH AND BEGINNING A CAREER

Catherine was headed to life in the North, this time as a young adult, but that would not mean a life free from second-class citizenship. Being a mulatto, or having bi-racial heritage, in Alabama, meant Black. Both Alabama and her ancestors' Georgia had adopted the "one drop rule" in 1927 for determining whether a person was White,[1] so any Black heritage in a person's ancestry, no matter how distant, legally classified that person as Black.

During her youth in the South, second-class treatment had remained endemic as the legacy of slavery and the Jim Crow heritage. With the African-American migration to the North and West in the post-Civil War era, second-class status followed. The situation had become national when Catherine was a young woman. As historian Peggy Pascoe notes, "By the 1920s, refusals to recognize the rights of African American women had become conventional in American law. So had refusals to recognize obvious inconsistencies in legal racial classification schemes."[2]

---

1 Peggy Pascoe, *What Comes Naturally* (New York: Oxford University Press, 2010), 119.
2 Peggy Pascoe, "Miscegenation Law, Court Cases, and Ideologies of 'race' in Twentieth-century America," *The Journal of American History*, Vol. 83, No. 1, June 1996, 52.

Part of the reason for this was the widespread acceptance in the late nineteenth century of "scientific racism," that combined Darwin's theory of evolution and its application to competition among races, known as "social Darwinism," with the pinnacle of belief in the supremacy of northern European races.[1] Scientific racism, that discussed competition among races in a Darwinian fashion, was further modified by the rediscovery of Mendel's work on dominant and recessive traits in the heredity of beans. The combination was seen to support the idea that behavior was the result of inherited nature, not social environment. The name it was given by Charles Darwin's cousin, Sir Francis Galton, was eugenics.[2]

Eugenics theories spread to all northern European countries and America. It was considered the science of improving human heredity in a way that was being done with livestock breeding, by encouraging the breeding of the "best" of human specimens and discouraging the breeding of others. To accomplish this everyone was assigned to racial categories, and each of these races was asserted to have both biological and social characteristics. The contention was that just as Mendel had demonstrated with beans, it was possible to breed humans for desirable qualities, both intellectual and social. In America this suited the Progressive Era of the time, with the faith in putting science in the service of advancing the betterment of the condition of man. Eugenics had the appearance of being scientific by classifying people according to a hierarchy, or taxonomy, to promote the breeding of a superior gene pool.

There were competing classifications, the most elaborate and influential compiled by the Dillingham Commission, a joint Senate–House of Representatives commission that was advised by eugenicist Dr. Henry Laughlin. Volume Five of the 40-volume report identified 600 branches and 45 distinct racial categories of immigrants in the U.S.[3] Briefly outlined, all hierarchical eugenics systems put what were considered the useless, the

1 John P. Jackson and Nadine M. Weidman, "The Origins of Scientific Racism," *The Journal of Blacks in Higher Education*, No. 50, Winter 2005/2006, 66.
2 Sally Satel, "A Better Breed of American," *New York Times*, Feb 26, 2006.
3 Arleen Marcia Tuchman, "Diabetes and Race, a Historical Perspective," *American Journal of Public Health*, Vol. 101, No.1, Jan 2011, 11.

epileptics, feebleminded, blind, deformed and disabled at the bottom. Next lowest were the Blacks. Above them came what were considered degenerate races, including the Jews, and the colored people of Latin America and Asia, who were beneath the Slavs and Mediterranean Europeans. All these were well below the Teutonic people of northern Europe. Anglo-Saxons ranked high among the Teutonic people, but in the U.S. the American Whites, a special breed of Anglo-Saxon, topped the entire complex racial-ethnic structure.[1]

In England the idea gained a following especially among the elite, including Winston Churchill,[2] and then soon spread to America, where followers included among others Republican President Theodore Roosevelt, who warned of "race suicide" if "inferior" races were to interbreed with Whites.[3] Segregationist Democratic President Woodrow Wilson[4] also was a eugenics proponent.[5] D.W. Griffin's film, *The Birth of a Nation*, had debuted two years before Catherine was born, and it remained the top feature length film until she had nearly finished high school. It earned praise from President Wilson.[6] Griffin said he called his film "The Birth of a Nation" because, "the real nation has only existed in the last fifteen or twenty years . . . The birth of a nation began . . . with the Ku Klux Klans."[7] Vice President Calvin Coolidge said in 1921, "Americans must be kept American. Biological laws show. . . that Nordics deteriorate when mixed with other races."[8]

---

1 For a more detailed discussion, see Dodge, *Andrea and Sylvester*, Ch. 3.
2 Satel, "A Better Breed of American".
3 "The Night President Teddy Roosevelt Invited Booker T. Washington to Dinner," *The Journal of Blacks in Higher Education*, No. 35, Spring 2002, 24.
4 "White supremacist ideology found fertile soil for growth in Wilson's progressive ideology," states B.T. Bates in his review of Eric S. Yellin's *Racism in the Nation's Service: Government Workers and the Color Line in Woodrow Wilson's America,* in *American Historical Review*, Vol.120, No. 3, 2015, 1048.
5 Paula Span, "How Did Woodrow Wilson Become America's Most Hated President?" *Historynet*, http://www.historynet.com/woodrow-wilson.
6 Arthur Lennig, "Myth and Fact: The Reception of 'The Birth of a Nation'," *Film History*, Vol. 16, No. 2, 2004, 120.
7 Michael Rogin, " 'The Sword Became a Flashing Vision': D.W. Griffin's The Birth of a Nation," *Representations*, No. 9, Winter 1985, 151.
8 Hiroshi Motomura, "Whose Alien Nation?: Two Models of

By the 1920s eugenics was embedded in the culture, as "better baby" contests were common at state fairs, while biology textbooks commonly included a eugenics chapter. A film from 1915, *The Black Stork*, where a doctor euthanized a child born with a birth defect, was shown to students in many schools.[1] When Catherine was in college, the *Los Angeles Times* Sunday magazine ran a column called "Social Eugenics." Its author Fred Hogue claimed, "In this country we have wiped out the mosquito carriers of yellow fever and are in a fair way to extinguish the malaria carriers; but the human breeders of the hereditary physical and mental unfit are only in exceptional cases placed under restraint."[2]

Eugenics won big victories nationally in the 1920s that Catherine's father would have known well, and she would have become aware of as the decade drew to an end. Passage of the Immigration Act of 1924 set strict quotas on what was frequently called the "new immigration" which had arrived more recently from Eastern and Southern Europe, was largely Catholic and included some Eastern European Jews, and severely restricted all immigrants from Black Africa. The "old immigrations" from northern Protestant Western Europe continued to be allowed in much larger numbers. It also completely eliminated all immigration from Asia,[3] which led a resurgent Japan to declare in July a National Humiliation Day with anti-American mass rallies focused on the institutionalization of racial inferiority inherent in the U.S. quota system.[4] The U.S. Supreme Court authorized involuntary sterilization of the feebleminded and other "defectives" in the 1927 case of *Buck v. Bell*,[5] a policy that was adopted by most states.

Constitutional Immigration Law," *Michigan Law Review*, Vol.94, No. 6, May 1996, 1930.

1 Steven Selden, "Transforming Better Babies into Fitter Families: Archival Resources and the History of the American Eugenics Movement, 1908-1930," *Proceedings of the American Philosophical Society*, Vol. 149, No. 2, June 2005, 205.

2 Fred Hogue, "Social Eugenics," *Los Angeles Times*, July 5, 1936, 29.

3 "The Immigration Act of 1924 (The Jonson-Reed Act)," U.S. Department of State Office of the Historian, http://history.state.gov/milestones/19211936/ImmigrationAct.

4 A. Warner Parker, "The Ineligible to Citizenship Provisions of the Immigration Act of 1924," *The American Journal of International Law*, Jan 1925.

5 *Buck v. Bell*, 274 U.S., 200.

In 1929, when Catherine could have been in Chicago with Hattie as a young girl, W.E.B. Du Bois debated Harvard PhD Theodore Stoppard in a public forum on the question, "Should the Negro be Encouraged to Cultural Equality?"[1] Stoppard asserted, "We know that our America is a White America . . . And the overwhelming weight of both historical and scientific evidence shows that only so long as the American people remain white will its institutions, ideals and culture continue to fit the temperament of its inhabitants—and hence continue to endure."[2]

Du Bois, in his rebuttal, spoke of the long-standing White fear of rape of their women that lead to the lynching of Blacks, and argued that it was much more likely that a White man would rape his sister. He continued, "We have not asked amalgamation[3]: we have resisted it. It has been forced on us by brute strength, ignorance, poverty, degradation, and fraud. It is the white race, roaming the world, that has left its trail of bastards and outraged women and then raised holy hands to heaven and deplored 'race mixture.'"[4]

While there is no way to know how this affected Catherine, it seems unlikely that it would have had no influence. Years later she said, "Ironically I found some of the same limitations in New York, Chicago, San Francisco and even Ann Arbor, Michigan, that I rejected in the South. Poverty and bigotry assume different forms and have many different objects. Bigotry may include ethnic groups, the poor, religious groups, or women."[5]

Catherine's marriage partnership was once described with what she would call, in her way of making comparisons, "shades of" eugenic approval.[6] Her enduring awareness of eugenics and the racism it promoted was indicated by a choice she made years later at North Dakota State University. Her selection of a speak-

1 Carol M. Taylor, "W.E.B. Du Bois's Challenge to Scientific Racism," *Journal of Black Studies* Vol. 11, No. 4, June 1981, 449.
2 Ibid.
3 Amalgamation was the traditional word for mixing of the races.
4 Taylor, "W.E.B. Du Bois's Challenge to Scientific Racism," 456.
5 Kosse, "Cater: 'infect one another with the desire to learn,' " 6.
6 "[The annual report [of the Rosewald Foundation] of 1943 commented on the Golightlys as an example of a "talented couple," Marianne A Ferber and Jane W Loeb, *Academic Couples: Problems and Promises*, (Urbana: University of Illinois Press, 1997), 90.

er to invite to address the students and faculty indicated her concern with eugenics attitudes and that she remained vigilant in countering them even when they had declined in popular and academic acceptance.[1]

Catherine arrived in Ann Arbor in the fall of 1938 as one of the 19,591 enrolled students at the University of Michigan.[2] She had from 2:00 to 2:15 on the afternoon of Friday, September 23, to register for her classes, and on Monday, September 26, began work on her master's degree.[3]

Along with her studies in English, she was writing poetry. Though it would soon be in print, she was always modest. Of her writing, she made self-deprecating comments, including, "I like to write verse. I don't say poetry. Verse is a lower level,"[4] and she was "not sure it was poetry, it was verse."[5]

Fees for Michigan graduate students were $75 per semester for nonresident students.[6] In the Depression, finding $150 to spend each year to attend school was not easy for all. To find work to help pay expenses, the university provided an employment office for men in the Dean of Students Office, while women desiring employment during college could obtain information by writing to the office of the Dean of Women. If women were interested in stenographic or clerical employment, there was a location where direct applications for "this class of employment may be filed."[7]

Catherine's background brought her in prepared for the rigorous academic expectations to earn a master's degree in English Language and Literature. To enter the program, students took a test on their critical thinking ability and their knowledge of

---

1 See chapter 10, Catherine's choice of Ashley Montagu for lecture series.

2 *University of Michigan: The President's Report for 1938-1939* (Ann Arbor, MI: University of Michigan, University of Michigan Official Publication, Ann Arbor, MI: University of Michigan Libraries), 211.

3 Ibid., 18.

4 "Excerpts: Catherine Cater," *NDSU Magazine*, Vol. 01, No.1, Fall, 2000, Catherine Cater Collection, Box 1, Folder 37, North Dakota State University Archives, Fargo, ND.

5 Vanorny, interview of Catherine Cater, Tape A.

6 *University of Michigan: The President's Report for 1938-1939*, 33.

7 Ibid., 43

the the important works of English authors, plus the important facts of English literary history.[1] One of the requirements for the degree was a reading knowledge of German or French, and she studied German to meet it.[2] The university stated that it "regards a knowledge of the ancient languages as highly desirable,"[3] which suited Catherine, who had mastered Greek along the way with her interest in philosophy and ancient mythology. Also, candidates were expected to be well prepared in English and foreign literature, in history, philosophy, and "other fundamental related subjects."[4] Beyond the course work, which had to include something in Old English, the dissertation was the final challenge.

Catherine did her course work for the duration of the school year, then found a job to help support herself when summer vacation came. Both school and vacation were learning experiences. For three summers, 1939–41, she worked in Wisconsin at a "camp for slum children,"[5] boys and girls whose ages ranged from five to 18, of diverse races and nationalities.[6] Catherine was naïve at the time. She recalled, "I was very innocent. I had never heard profanity such as these children used. I didn't even know how to spell some of their words!"[7] During her first summer, her main job was to teach rowing, even though she did not know how to swim.[8] Other summers she taught puppeteering and typing.[9] For reasons she did not share, she kept her job a secret from her father.[10] The psychologist that worked with the camp project was Theodore Dreikurs, who, Catherine said, believed the "idea that every child needs a sense of self-esteem."[11]

---

1 *University of Michigan: The Horace H. Rackham School of Graduate Studies, Announcement 1939–1940* (Ann Arbor, MI: University of Michigan, University of Michigan Official Publication, Ann Arbor, MI: University of Michigan Libraries, 1940)162.
2 Paul Homan interview.
3 Ibid.
4 Ibid.
5 Vanorny, interview of Catherine Cater, Tape A.
6 Hanson, "Catherine Cater," 21.
7 Ibid.
8 Vanorny, interview of Catherine Cater, Tape A.
9 Ibid.
10 Ibid.
11 Hanson, "Catherine Cater," 21.

Dreikurs did important work in education research, and she learned new theories of teaching children from working with him.[1] He is known for contributing to "positive discipline," believing teachers needed to be "leaders rather than bosses," also making a distinction between encouragement, which he viewed positively, and praise.[2] He stressed "logical consequences" rather than punishment as a form of discipline, where a child saw that actions have consequences but self-worth was supported. An example of this given for classroom use with young children is the difference between the following two teacher responses for dealing with the same situation of a child marking on his desk when he was meant to be coloring on a piece of paper:

"I saw you mark on that table. You get a sponge and clean the marks off, young man, on this table and the other two."

"Looks like your marker went off the paper. Let's get a sponge and clean it off before it dries."

While an adult may see response "a" as a "logical consequence," it would most likely be perceived by a child as a punishment. Choice "b" teaches that the child's actions have logical consequences, but also supports his self-worth.[3] Encouragement would certainly become a hallmark of Catherine's interaction with students, and this experience with Dreikurs may have been in some way a contributing factor to her adopting that style.

Catherine wrote her master's thesis on John Keats' 1818 poem "Endymion,"[4] known for its opening line, "A thing of beauty is a joy forever." This brought together Catherine's abiding interests in literature and classical mythology. Endymion was a beautiful youth in Greek mythology who spent his life beyond youth in perpetual sleep in a cave, remaining ever youthful. Selene, the goddess of the moon, loved him and visited him nightly while he slept, and bore him 50 daughters.[5] There has been considerable

---

1 "Finding Aid to the Catherine Cater Papers," Biography, NDSU Institute for Regional Studies & Universities Archives, North Dakota State University, Fargo ND, 2.
2 Dan Gartrell, *A Guidance Approach for the Encouraging Classroom* (Belmont, CA: Wadsworth Publishing Co, 2013), 15.
3 Gartrell, *A Guidance Approach*, 240-241.
4 Poem available at http://www.bartleby.com/126/32.html.
5 "Endymion, Greek Mythology," *Encyclopedia Britannica*, http://www.britannica.com/topic/Endymion-Greek-mythology.

scholarly discussion of the poem, and whether it was an allegory, Platonic or Neo-Platonic.[1]

Catherine's efforts were sufficient to satisfy her committee, and she graduated with a Master of Arts Degree in English Literature. There is some disagreement on the date, as the "Biography" in the Finding Aid to the Catherine Cater Papers has her graduating in 1939,[2] but the University of Michigan commencement bulletin puts it as the spring of 1941.[3] The university's register for students listed her as an unspecified graduate student for the 1938–39 school year[4] and she appears on their list of graduates in their general registrar for 1939.[5] The dates are further complicated by the fact that she is recorded as having completed a library degree in the spring of 1940,[6] and her interviews indicate that she began library school after she had finished her master's degree but had been unable to secure employment. The year that makes sense in this context is 1939. Perhaps her inclusion on the 1941commencement bulletin was as a matter of convenience, enabling her to attend the ceremony, or is just a mistake; either way, evidence from other sources makes it clear that by that time she no longer was in Michigan.

In the two extended interviews Catherine gave, she described returning to summer camp one final time and the lasting affect it had on her. In her 1983 interview, Nancy Hanson reported that Catherine was asked to make follow-up calls at the homes of some of the campers in Chicago "at the end of the final

---

1 For a discussion of various interpretations see Glen O. Allen, "The Fall of Endymion: A Study in Keats's Intellectual Growth," *Keats-Shelley Journal*, Vol. 6, Winter 1957.

2 *Finding Aid to the Catherine Cater Papers*, "Biography," NDSU Institute for Regional Studies & University Archives, http://library.ndsu.edu/repository/bitstream/handle/10365/377/Cater,CatherinePapers.pdf, 2.

3 *Ninety-Seventh Commencement*, University of Michigan (Ann Arbor, MI: University of Michigan, University of Michigan Official Publication, June 21, 1941), 51.

4 *University of Michigan: The President's Report for 1938-1939*, Volume 41(Ann Arbor, MI: University of Michigan, University of Michigan Official Publications, 1939), 82.

5 *General Registrar: University of Michigan* (Ann Arbor Michigan: University of Michigan), University of Michigan Official Publication,1939, 155.

6 *Register of Staff and Graduates* (Ann Arbor Michigan: University of Michigan), University of Michigan Official Publication, July 1 1939, through June 30, 1940, Vol. 42, No. 81, 141.

summer,"[1] which would have been 1940. Catherine said, "The ad-dresses were in the heart of the Chicago slums. I didn't know enough to be fearful . . . I worked and worked with one woman, trying to figure out the relationship between her income and expenses. Finally I told her, 'I just can't make these come out even.' She patted me on my sailor-hatted head and said, 'Honey, you sure are young.' "[2] Speaking with Hannah Vanorny in 2005, Catherine told of being sent to Chicago tenements during her summer job, where she first met a prostitute. Also she spoke of visiting a home and talking to a boy who had pinned the ear of another boy to a wall. Her experience was significant, since she had always said she "would never, never be a teacher,"[3] but this visit had convinced her she could not become a social worker.[4] It appears we may have to thank some misbehaved boy in Chicago years ago, as the unintended consequences of his behavior left Catherine with no choice but to become a teacher, to the great benefit of so many people in the years to come.

Hanson reports that Catherine looked for a job in an inte-grated college or university, and thought, "Perhaps I might have found a job in the South, but I didn't want to capitulate with a segregated institution."[5] She added, "Shades of today—no jobs for women, especially Black women in higher education."

Catherine had two barriers to overcome in seeking to break into the White university system: the assumptions that women were not college teachers and African-Americans were not col-lege teachers. She took a scholarship to the University of Michi-gan library school to gain a credential where poorly paid jobs existed. She recalled, "I cordially disliked the whole curriculum. But it was a lifesaver—my admission to the universities."[6] And that it would be, but there is a story that receives little coverage, and what is included was incompletely told to the interviewers at best.

---

1 Hanson, "Catherine Cater," 21.
2 Ibid.
3 Vanorny, interview of Catherine Cater, Tape A.
4 Ibid.
5 Ibid., 22.
6 Hanson, "Catherine Cater," 22.

Hannah Vanorny reported that Catherine married a graduate school classmate, a philosophy major.[1] It is true that Catherine was romantically involved with someone who was attending the same graduate school, but that was not where they met. She had known him and been in school with him since their undergraduate college days at Talladega in Alabama.[2] Cornelius Golightly and Catherine both graduated in 1938, and he was a most unusual man.

Cornelius Golightly was the youngest of three children born to Reverend Richmond Golightly, and the former Margaret, Maggy, Catherine Fullilove of Holmes County, Mississippi. Both parents were recorded as a Negroes by census takers.[3] His father was listed as a self-employed minister on his World War I draft card[4] and a Presbyterian clergyman on the 1930 census.[5] In 1940 Reverend Golightly was a minister in the "protestant church."[6] At Talladega College, Cornelius Golightly was a scholar-athlete, participating in football, baseball and tennis, while being one of only five Black students from across the nation to earn honors in the 1938 academic competition "Intellectual Olympics."[7] Both he and Catherine left Talladega and headed to the University of Michigan in 1938, and whether that was coincidental is unknown. At Michigan he finished his master's in philosophy degree in his first year, and when 1939 came to a close he received

---

1 Vanorny, interview of Catherine Cater, Tape B.

2 "Dr. Cornelius Golightly (1917–1976): The Life of an Academic and Public Intellectual," *BlackPast.org*, http://www.blackpast.org/perspectives/dr-cornelius-golightly-1917-1976-life-academic-and-public-intellectual.

3 *Fifteenth Census of the United States, 1930*, United States of America, Bureau of the Census, Washington, D.C.: National Archives and Records Administration, 1930. T626, Laurel, Jones, Mississippi; Roll: 1151; Page: 42A; Enumeration District: 0010; Image: 877.0; FHL microfilm: 2340886.

4 *World War I Selective Service System Draft Registration Cards, 1917–1918*, United States, Selective Service System, Washington, D.C.: National Archives and Records Administration, M1509, Mississippi; Registration County: Marshall; Roll: 1682940.

5 *Fifteenth Census of the United States, 1930*.

6 *Sixteenth Census of the United States, 1940*, United States of America, Bureau of the Census, Washington, D.C.: National Archives and Records Administration, 1940. T627, Atlanta, Fulton, Georgia; Roll: T627_726; Page: 9B; Enumeration District: 160-61.

7 "Dr. Cornelius Golightly (1917-1976): The Life of an Academic and Public Intellectual."

national attention for winning an essay contest sponsored by The New History Society.[1] Winning the contest brought a $300 prize and stories in papers nationally. The *Pittsburgh Courier*, with a banner headline that said "Young Negro . . . Shows Qualities,"[2] wrote a detailed story of Golightly's background of playing three years of varsity football while spending summers working, picking cotton, and serving as a busboy and waiter on steamers as an undergraduate. He had become a graduate assistant by his second semester at Michigan, and in his second year he was working on a PhD. The *New York Age* gave little more than the title of Golightly's essay in its article, "History Essay Prize Won by Former Cotton Picker."[3]

Following the 1940 school year, Catherine was a certified librarian in search of entry into the academic world. Her opportunity came when she was offered what has previously been reported as the position as head of the circulation department of the library at Fisk University,[4] in Nashville, Tennessee. In fact, she was a librarian but she did not become head of the circulation department until her final year at Fisk. The Nashville city directory listed her address as 913 18th Avenue North and described her as a librarian. Her name was followed by a (c) to indicate that she was "colored."[5]

It was her first full time job, and she also taught sections of freshman English. She had her foot in the door. Catherine recalled, "I disliked the city intensely. It was one of the smoggiest places in the nation at the time, and there was segregation everywhere. I'd been pretty sheltered all my life, you know, up on that hill in Alabama."[6]

The fact that Catherine started her teaching career at Fisk had special meaning to African-American Dr. Yvonne Condell, a legendary teacher at Moorhead State University in Minnesota,

1 "Young Negro Student Wins $300.00 Award: Takes 1st Prize in National Contest; University of Michigan Student Shows Qualities in Contest," *Pittsburgh Courier*, December 23, 1939, 14.
2 Ibid.
3 "History Essay Prize Won by Former Cotton Picker," The *New York Age*, (New York), Dec 9, 1939, 3.
4 See Homan, "A Humanist in Honors," 88.
5 "Cater A Cath," *Nashville, Tennessee City Directory*, 1941, 101.
6 Hanson, "Catherine Cater," 22.

who is one of Catherine's detractors. She commented, "It explains her for me. Fisk is an elitist school for African-Americans, very elitist. The two African-American institutions that were elitist were Howard University and Fisk. So she started out in an elitist environment and just continued with it. For me that explains her and her demeanor . . . because she started out at a very elitist place, Fisk. She was a complex person. She wasn't easy to categorize."[1]

Fisk had been established six months after the end of the Civil War in former Union Army barracks with students who had endured slavery and poverty and ranged in age from seven to 70. It was named for General Clinton Fisk of the Tennessee Freedmen's Bureau. In 1867 it was incorporated and the American Missionary Association was involved in its development, with the affiliation of the original founders. Its statement of purpose said that the institution would be measured by "the highest standards, not of Negro education, but of American education at its best."[2] Fisk was the first African-American institution accredited by the Southern Association of Colleges and Schools and the first on the approved list of the Association of American Universities.[3] Not long after Catherine's time there, it would become the first African-American institution approved by the American Association of University Women,[4] an organization in which Catherine would become active and Yvonne Condell would become a national leader during her more than 50 years of active membership.[5]

W.E.B. Du Bois was a Fisk graduate and Booker T. Washington served on the board of trustees, while his wife was a graduate as were his children. There were Pulitzer Prize winners and others in the arts, including Arna Bontemps, who would be instrumental in seeing Catherine's poetry in print repeatedly. Many civil rights leaders are associated with the institution,

---

1 Yvonne Condell, interview with Robert Dodge, Moorhead, MN, Oct 11, 2015.
2 "Fisk University History," *Fisk University*, http://www.fisk.edu/about/history.
3 Ibid.
4 Ibid.
5 See "Changing Her World," *Leaving a Legacy*, aauw.stelter.com/assets/stelter-pdf/Legacy3_6140.pdf.

including the first African-American Supreme Court Justice, Thurgood Marshall, who attended the school's Race Relations Institute, and alumnus U.S. Representative from Georgia, John Lewis,[1] the former Freedom Rider and head of the Student Nonviolent Coordinating Committee (SNCC) who was one of the speakers at the March on Washington in 1963.[2] The university had a heritage of historic and cultural achievement in the African-American population.

In the fall of 1940, during her first month as a college faculty member, Catherine was already volunteering to work with students. She wrote to Fisk President Thomas Jones that she would be "very happy to serve to the best of my ability as an advisor for the year 1940–41. The actively creative advisory system should be of great value to both student and faculty participants."[3]

While Catherine was at Fisk, Cornelius Golightly received a Rosenwald Fellowship and completed his doctorate in 1941. He would continue to use the fellowship to do post-doctorate studies at Harvard.[4] Throughout this time, their long distance relationship had obviously been growing more serious, as on August 5, 1941, in Chicago, Catherine and Cornelius were married.[5]

The Cook County, Illinois, county clerk filed their license on August 7, making it official, and Catherine listed herself as from Nashville, Tennessee, as the wedding did not bring them together permanently. Thus began a most unusual marriage. There is no record of Catherine having accompanying Cornelius to Harvard for any extended period.

Two years after Catherine got her start at Fisk, her husband, Cornelius, began a teaching career. The chair of the philosophy department at Howard University invited Catherine's husband to teach philosophy and social science for the academic year

---

1 "Fisk University History".
2 "Biography," *Congressman John Lewis*, https://johnlewis.house.gov/john-lewis/biography.
3 Catherine Cater, letter to President Thomas Jones of Fisk University, Sept 20, 1940, *Fisk University, John Hope and Aurelia E. Franklin Library, Special Collections*, Series IV: Faculty and Staff Subseries I: Correspondence and Contracts, Box 16, folder 50, Cater, Catherine, 1940.
4 Ferber and Loeb, *Academic Couples*, 90.
5 Cook County Clerk, comp, *Cook County Clerk Genealogy Records*, Cook County Clerk's Office, Chicago, IL: Cook County Clerk, Marriage License, No. 1693478, filed Aug 7, 1951, 2008.

1942–43.[1] On April 21, 1942, Catherine received an offer of an advancement at Fisk. President Jones wrote to her:

> My dear Mrs. Golightly:
>
> The Trustees of Fisk University have authorized me to state that you have been appointed CIRCULATIONS LIBRARIAN at Fisk University for the year beginning July 1st 1942 and ending June 30th 1943.
> The allowance is Fifteen Hundred Dollars ($1500.00). Your checks to be paid in twelve (12) monthly instalments. The Trustees reserve the right to reduce this salary if required by circumstances due to the present emergency.
>
> Please indicate your acceptance by signing your name on the line provided below.[2]

Catherine signed with the curious signature, "Catherine Cater (Golightly)."[3]

Catherine took on her new responsibility by immediately becoming involved in campus affairs. She and President Jones exchanged letters about a student newspaper that began with him writing, "Every year about this time a question is raised regarding the best method of making available various announcements and news items to faculty, students, and others in this community."[4] He explained that there had at one time been a weekly newspaper, and that critics of the current announcement sheet, "The Clarion," would like to see it "have a little more of a newspaper flavor."[5] He was forming a committee and hoped that she would participate. Catherine responded the follow-

---

1 "Dr. Cornelius Golightly (1917-1976): The Life of an Academic and Public Intellectual."

2 Thomas E. Jones, letter to Catherine Cater Golightly, April, 21,1942, *Fisk University, John Hope and Aurelia E. Franklin Library, Special Collections*, Series IV: Faculty and Staff Subseries I: Correspondence and Contracts, Box 17, folder 18, Golightly, Catherine (Cater), 1942-1943.

3 Ibid.

4 Thomas E. Jones, letter to Catherine Cater Golightly, October 13,1942, *Fisk University, John Hope and Aurelia E. Franklin Library, Special Collections*, Series IV: Faculty and Staff Subseries I: Correspondence and Contracts, Box 17, folder 18, Golightly, Catherine (Cater), 1942-1943.

5 Ibid.

ing day by writing that she would "be very happy to have the privilege of serving as a member of the committee,"[1] and added, "Several students have expressed interest in working with a current campus newspaper, and an investigation along this line is certainly well worthwhile."[2]

Later that month President Jones again wrote to Catherine, addressing her as "My Dear Miss Cater,"[3] to congratulate her on an article she had written for *The Library Journal*. He commented, "Such articles are of value to Fisk and also to the contributor."[4] This was the first time he addressed her using the name "Cater," but it is more interesting that she had become "Miss," presumably because of her insistence to not go by her husband's name, other than in parenthesis.

Marianne A. Ferber and Jane W. Loeb wrote that, "Cornelius earned his doctorate in 1941 and continued studies in religion at Harvard University. Catherine was employed at Fisk University during this period, but applied for a second fellowship to complete her doctorate while Cornelius was employed on the faculty of Howard University,"[5] This is an incomplete telling of the story. Even while Cornelius was at Harvard, evidence indicates he had become more than a student and had already begun doing what would be his part for the war effort. While he would get one year in at Howard, large events had taken charge.

World War II had begun in 1939 and the U.S. was to be drawn in. The demand for workers would increase dramatically, just as much of the work force would enlist or face conscription. The president of the Brotherhood of Sleeping Car Porters had met with Eleanor Roosevelt and members of the President's cabinet to present a list of grievances for the civil rights of Blacks in America. He and others were planning a march on Washing-

---

1 Catherine Cater, letter to Thomas E. Jones, October 14,1942, *Fisk University, John Hope and Aurelia E. Franklin Library, Special Collections*, Series IV: Faculty and Staff Subseries I: Correspondence and Contracts, Box 17, folder 18, Golightly, Catherine (Cater), 1942–1943.
2 Ibid.
3 Thomas E. Jones, letter to Catherine Cater, October 31,1942, *Fisk University, John Hope and Aurelia E. Franklin Library, Special Collections*, Series IV: Faculty and Staff Subseries I: Correspondence and Contracts, Box 17, folder 18, Golightly, Catherine (Cater), 1942-1943.
4 Ibid.
5 Ferber and Loeb, *Academic Couples*, 90.

ton that would bring "ten, twenty, fifty-thousand Negroes on the White House lawn" if changes weren't made.[1] President Roosevelt responded in June 1941 with Executive Order 8802 that stated, "There shall be no discrimination in the employment of workers in defense industries and in Government, because of race, creed, color, or national origin."[2] For the first time since post Civil War Reconstruction, a Presidential directive on race had been announced. The planned march on Washington was cancelled.

Stanford Historian David Kennedy notes that the United States "erected the factories and recruited the workers necessary to pour out the greatest arsenal of weaponry the world had ever seen."[3] To do this required bringing in previously forbidden workers to assembly lines, including Blacks and women. Helping oversee the assimilation of the Black workers in the formerly segregated workforce was a heavy responsibility for a 26-year-old Cornelius, and he took it on from 1943 until the War's end in 1945. He did this as a Compliance Analyst with the Fair Employment Practices Committee.[4] His biography[5] states that he took this work on after his year at Howard in 1943, but "Reports from the Special Services Divisions" indicate that he had actually begun the work earlier, while a student at Harvard, shortly after the U.S. entered the War.[6]

Catherine and Cornelius were living parallel lives. Catherine received a fellowship and had an opportunity to return to Michigan to pursue her PhD. She submitted her resignation letter to Fisk on April 18, 1943. It would be the first and most

---

1 Beth Tompkins Bates, *Pullman Porters and the Rise of Protest Politics in Black America, 1925–1945* (Chapel Hill, NC: The University of North Carolina Press, 2001), 158-160.
2 http://www.archives.gov/historical-docs/todays-doc/?dod-date=625.
3 David M. Kennedy, *Freedom from Fear: The American People in Depression and War, 1929–1945* (New York: Oxford University Press, 1999), 655.
4 "Dr. Cornelius Golightly (1917–1976): The Life of an Academic and Public Intellectual."
5 Ibid.
6 Richard M. Dalfiume, "The 'Forgotten Years' of the Negro Revolution," *The Journal of American History*, Vol. 55, No. 1, Jun1968, 102, Note 58, "Reports from the Special Services Division Submitted April 23, 1942: Negro Organizations and the War Effort," Cornelius Golightly, "Negro Morale in Boston," Special Services Division Report No. 7, May 19, 1942.

amiable of her three resignations from universities. Her letter to University President Thomas Jones stated: "It is with sincerity that I express to you my appreciation of the opportunity which I have had to serve as a faculty member at Fisk University during the past three years. The contacts, with colleagues and with students, the work itself, have proved enlightening and in many cases, vitalizing. I only regret that I have no more to contribute to the institution."[1] She expressed "Best wishes for an effective and dynamic education program in this changing world of ours."[2]

President Jones' response indicates that Catherine's initial foray into higher education had been a success. Again calling her "Miss Cater," he replied, "As you leave me no alternative, I am herewith accepting this resignation. I think you know that I do this with keen regret, as is evidenced by the rapid advancement both in position and salary which we have accorded you during your stay at Fisk. I recognize that your love of English and your desire to complete your graduate work in this field are worthy ambitions and can only receive our encouragement."[3]

It was 1943 and she was moving from the South permanently, but there was a part of it she would take with her that would make her distinctive. She would never be a reserved, stoic Northerner. People who have been in her classes, or her friends, have seen her warm, natural gestures, as she described: "It's a habit. I was born in New Orleans, you know. When I go there now I see that I'm surrounded by others who smile constantly, wave their hands around when they talk as I do and easily laugh or cry."[4]

1 Catherine Cater, letter to Thomas E. Jones, April 18, 1943, *Fisk University, John Hope and Aurelia E. Franklin Library, Special Collections*, Series IV: Faculty and Staff Subseries I: Correspondence and Contracts, Box 17, folder 18, Golightly, Catherine (Cater), 1942-1943.
2 Ibid.
3 Thomas E. Jones, letter to Catherine Cater, April 23,1943, *Fisk University, John Hope and Aurelia E. Franklin Library, Special Collections*, Series IV: Faculty and Staff Subseries I: Correspondence and Contracts, Box 17, folder 18, Golightly, Catherine (Cater), 1942-1943.
4 Hanson, "Catherine Cater," 19.

CHAPTER 6. MICHIGAN LIFE, UPS AND DOWNS

Catherine left Fisk and returned to Ann Arbor as, in the words of her close friend, Paul Homan, "a young person in a great hurry."[1] She was able to afford this move since, for a second time;[2] she was the recipient of a Rosenwald Fellowship.

The Rosenwald Foundation's purpose, as stated in its charter, was the "well-being of mankind."[3] Its founder, Julius Rosenwald, believed that would that all humankind would benefit from the education of African-Americans. He clarified, "I am interested in the Negro people because I am also interested in the white people. Negros are one-tenth of our population. If we promote better citizenship among the Negroes not only are they improved, but our entire citizenship is benefitted."[4] The primary focus of the foundation was on building schools in rural areas of the South and activities centered on welfare and education of African-Americans. By the late 1920s the foundation began granting fellowships for higher education in four areas: physicians and nurses, teachers of vocational subjects, special teachers such as librarians and music teachers, individuals of promise

---

1 Homan, "A Humanist in Honors," 88.
2 Ferber and Loeb, *Academic Couples*, 90.
3   J. Scott McCormick, "The Julius Rosenwald Fund," *The Journal of Negro Education* Vol.3, No.4, Oct 1934, 605.
4 Ibid.

in any subject.[1] Clearly, the fellowships for Catherine and her husband had fallen in the final category.

In Ann Arbor Catherine settled in at 616 North 5th Avenue.[2] There, and at the University of Michigan, she began examining the influence of Platonism in Milton and soon had an article published on Southern poets.[3] During this time she was interviewed for a fellowship by Lillian Smith, who Catherine later singled out to Hannah Vanorny as a person she admired, along with Langston Hughes.[4] These are interesting choices that tell us a bit more about Catherine.

Nancy Edmonds wrote that Hughes had been an "obvious influence" on Catherine's father,[5] without explaining why it was obvious. Hughes was a major figure of the Harlem Renaissance of the 1920s and early 30s when Black art flourished in America. His prose and poetry spoke of the lives of everyday African-Americans, and he called for racial pride along with artistic expression. As he became more experimental, he focused on "the ordinary Negroes [who] hadn't heard of the Negro Renaissance."[6] After writing his second book of poems, *Fine Clothes to the Jew*,[7] he said it was well received in literary magazines but Negro critics did not like it; and he was labeled "The poet 'low-rate' [rather than laureate] of Harlem."[8] There were some who called the book "a disgrace to the race"[9] for parading racial defects before the public. His work certainly stood the test of time, as Princeton Professor Wallace Best attests, "Langston Hughes stands as one of the most important American writers of the last century."[10]

1 Ibid., 624.
2 "Cater, Althea C.," *Ann Arbor, Michigan, City Directory*, 1945, 72.
3 Homan, "A Humanist in Honors," 88.
4 Vanorny, interview of Catherine Cater, Tape A.
5 Hanson, "Catherine Cater," 21.
6 "Langston Hughes: a Biography," *Masterpiece Theatre/American Collection/ Cora Unashamed*, http://www.pbs.org/wgbh/masterpiece/americancollection/cora/ei_hughesbiography.html.
7 Langston Hughes, *Fine Clothes to the Jew* (New York: A. A. Knoff, 1929).
8 Langston Hughes, *The Big Sea: An Autobiography* (New York: Hill and Wang, 2015), 266.
9 Ibid.
10 Wallace Best, "Celebrating Black History Month – Langston Hughes," *Center for African American Studies, Princeton University*, https://www.princeton.edu/africanamericanstudies/news/archive/index.xml?id=9594, Feb 12, 2014.

It is unclear what Catherine admired about Hughes, whether it was his prolific body of work, his giving voice to the spirit of Harlem, his great success as an African-American poet, or his being an early champion for civil rights who used his writing to support equality for women, Blacks, workers, the socially disadvantaged.[1] Perhaps in part it was that he recognized her significance. The time was not far off when he would request a piece of her "verse" for inclusion in an anthology of Negro poetry.

While Hughes might have been anticipated as someone Catherine admired in her younger days, her singling out Smith for such praise is more provocative. Smith was "one of the first prominent white Southerners to denounce racial segregation openly and to work actively against the entrenched and often brutally enforced world of Jim Crow. From as early as the 1930s, she argued that Jim Crow was evil."[2] Her highly provocative and successful book *Strange Fruit*[3] was released the year after Catherine returned to Michigan. This book tells the story of an interracial romance set in fictional Maxwell, Georgia, in the 1920s. In the narrative the community was divided into "White Town" and "Colored Town." The lovers were Tracy Deen, a White college dropout from a prominent, pretentious family, and Nonnie Anderson, an attractive, college educated light-skinned Black girl. They had been engaged in sex since she was 14 and he was 20, and events came to a head when Nonnie became pregnant. Tracy talked to his minister, who counseled him to "find some good nigger you can count on to marry her,"[4] and suggested that he offer to pay someone to accept the arrangement. With the help of some cash, Tracy convinced one of his family's servants, Henry, to futilely ask Nonnie to marry him. Nonnie's successful brother was in town and overheard what was happening, and he learned that Tracy was the father of Nonnie's baby. He became enraged and shot Tracy, then fled the town. "White Town" wanted a suspect and it needed to be a Black man. Slow-witted Henry had an alibi, but he was lynched and burnt to death.

---

1 Ibid.
2 Bruce *New Georgia Encyclopedia*, online http:www.georgiaencyclopedia.org/articles/arts-culture/Lillian-smith-1897-1966, Sept 1, 2015.
3 Lillian Smith, *Strange Fruit* (New York: Reynal & Hitchcock, 1944).
4 Ibid., 100.

The following day everything had returned to its old routine as though nothing had happened.[1] The book drew to a close with, "Everything would be the same—as it always was."[2]

This book was popular but very controversial. It was banned in Boston and Detroit shortly after its release, making it the first number one bestseller banned in Boston.[3] It was barred briefly from being shipped through the mail until its publisher convinced Eleanor Roosevelt to encourage her husband to lift the ban.[4] There was also controversy over the title, with Ms. Smith saying she chose "strange fruit" to refer to the "damaged, twisted people who are the products of our racist culture."[5] Singer Billie Holiday claimed Smith named the book after her hauntingly powerful song of the same name, "Strange Fruit," that she had developed from a poem by Abel Meeropol, a Jewish schoolteacher from the Bronx. He had written his verse in 1937 after seeing photographs of lynchings that were common in the South.[6] This was the poem he wrote and set to music, which a New York club owner gave to Holiday:[7]

> Southern trees bear a strange fruit,
> Blood on the leaves and blood at the root,
> Black body swinging in the Southern breeze,
> Strange fruit hanging from the poplar trees.
> Pastoral scene of the gallant South,
> The bulging eyes and the twisted mouth,
> Scent of magnolia sweet and fresh,
> And the sudden smell of burning flesh!
> Here is a fruit for the crows to pluck,
> For the rain to gather, for the wind to suck,

1 Summary of story from Dawn B. Sova, *Literature Suppressed on Social Grounds* (New York: Facts on File, 2006), 264-265.
2 Smith, *Strange Fruit*, 371.
3 Eric Z. Bass, "The Strange Life of Strange Fruit," Deep South Magazine online, http://deepsouthmag.com/2012/the-strange-life-of-strange-fruit/, Dec 12, 2012.
4 Smith Booklist, "Strange Fruit Book Review, Summary".
5 Ibid.
6 Emily Glaser, "The Song of the Century: Billie Holiday's 'Strange Fruit'," *PorterBriggs.Com: The Voice of the South*, http://porterbriggs.com/billie-holiday-strange-fruit/.
7 Elizabeth Blair, "The Strange Story of the Mane Behind 'Strange Fruit'," NPR Music, http://www.npr.org/2012/09/05/158933012/the-strange-story-of-the-man-behind-strange-fruit, Sept 5, 2012.

> For the sun to rot, for a tree to drop,
> Here is a strange and bitter crop.

Holiday's mother warned her not to sing it but Billie thought it might do some good, to which her mother replied, "—but you'll be dead."[1] When it was released, many radio stations banned it, including the BBC.[2] Billie Holiday's song had come out in 1939,[3] the same year as *Gone with the Wind*, which "embodied contemporary condescension toward blacks and black performers."[4] There can be little doubt that Catherine listened to this song, given how much attention it received and how well the record of it sold.[5] Holiday was a top star, and not only in the African-American community. She was featured in *Life* magazine in 1943 and given *Esquire* magazine's Gold award as best female vocalist in 1944.[6] But it was this song that really put her in the national spotlight.[7] One can only wonder what went through Catherine's mind and the emotions she felt when listening to Holiday sing of what she had witnessed in her youth.

The House of Representatives had passed an anti-lynching bill in 1935, and again in 1940, only to have it buried in the Senate both times. In both cases the bills lacked the support of President Franklin D. Roosevelt, who refused to endorse the legislation because he feared antagonizing Southern Democrats.[8] Holiday's song was courageous and influential, and it was eventually named by *Time* magazine as the "Song of the Century" in its final edition of 1999.[9]

Lillian Smith hadn't finished when she wrote her book *Strange Fruit*, for five years later she "hurled another thunderbolt

1 "Sold on Song: Strange Fruit," *BBC*, http://www.bbc.co.uk/radio2/soldonsong/songlibrary/indepth/strangefruit.shtml.
2 Ibid.
3 To hear it from her younger days: https://www.youtube.com/watch?v=0mO92ll_q0k, videos of her singing lit later in later life available on You Tube.
4 David Nassaw, "Show-Stopper: Strange Fruit: Billie Holiday, Café Society, and an Early Cry for Civil Rights," *New York Times*, May 21, 2000.
5 "Strange Fruit:1939," The Pop History Dig, http://www.pophistorydig.com/topics/tag/billie-holiday-1940s/.
6 Ibid.
7 Ibid.
8 Nassaw, "Show-Stopper".
9 Josh Sarburn, "Strange Fruit," *Time* online, Oct 21, 2011.

against racism"[1] when *Killers of the Dream*[2] was released. This was an explicit attack on all manifestations of Southern racism, including the Ku Klux Klan, lynching, sharecropping and segregation.[3] Smith also analyzed the relations between White men and Black women and their mulatto children, the "haunted Southern society."[4]

That Catherine chose to name these individuals as people she admired is especially informative as it came in 2005, when she was 88, and had been a longtime resident of Fargo-Moorhead. By that time, she had long since made a decision about her past that abandoned much about racial discord. But it was clearly being repressed and not forgotten. The figures she named as mattering most to her had been early outspoken champions of African-Americans who were victims in society. In her early years she had been exposed to Ku Klux Klan violence and had witnessed a Klan hanging. This was when she became the head of her college NAACP. While she was to step back from identifying herself as African-American, it is evident that her past had not been forgotten, and Smith had addressed mulattoes and their confused identity in Southern society where Catherine had grownup. How these dynamics would work as her life changed was part of her unfolding story.

She brought the South with her to Michigan when she worked on her doctorate degree. That Catherine's concern for social problems intermingled with her academic scholarship was evident in the choice of her thesis topic. Her PhD thesis had the title "Contemporary Southern Writers." She selected five: Caroline Gordoy, William Faulkner, Ellen Glasgow, T.S. Stribling, and Erkine Caldwell. Her issue was their individual approaches to social problems. In a rigorously researched and documented paper, she concluded on page 232 that their approaches to social problems "are significant for Southern thought in that they reveal a growing consciousness of social

1 Clayton, "Lillian Smith (1897-1966)".
2 Lillian Smith, *Killers of the Dream* (New York: W.W. Norton, 1949).
3 John C. Inscoe, "Killers of the Dream," New Georgia Encyclopedia, http://www.georgiaencyclopedia.org/articles/arts-culture/killers-dream, Aug 22, 2013.
4 Ibid.

problems which have been ignored by Southern writers of both fiction and non-fiction."[1]

With her PhD and limited experience at Fisk, Catherine landed a position as an English instructor at Olivet College beginning in the 1945–46 school year.[2] This was a considerable achievement, with her race and her gender as challenges that that few could overcome. Sharon Harley's book points out that, in the 1940s, even at "Negro colleges, married women were rarely given full faculty appointments and single women's pay was often lower than men's pay."[3] Harley mentions a woman who took a position at Oakwood College in Alabama, where she was the only PhD on the faculty, who overheard another faculty member thanking the college president for a raise. She asked him why she had not received one and was told, "Because you are a woman."[4] Catherine would find that a daunting problem in the world of higher education.

She was closer to her husband physically, and perhaps emotionally, during this time. After his years with the Fair Employment Practices Committee, he had moved to academia and also taken a position following World War II at Olivet College, at the same time Catherine joined the institution. Whether hiring them as a couple aided her is unknown. It was seen as a historic moment when Catherine's husband accepted this position, since for the first time in the twentieth century a Black philosopher had been hired as a faculty member in a philosophy department of a non-Black school.[5]

Olivet was a good match for Catherine, and her style as a teacher developed there. The small liberal arts college in Olivet, Michigan, was established in 1844, and its Congregational founders wrote as their guiding principle: "We wish simply to do good to our students, by placing in their hands the means

---

1 Catherine Cater, *Thesis* for Doctorate in English Language and Literature, University of Michigan, 1945, 232.
2 Her biography in *The Poetry of the Negro* (Garden City, New York: Doubleday& Company, 1951), 392, lists her as "librarian-instructor".
3 Sharon Harley, *Sister Circle: Black Women and Work* (New Brunswick, NJ: Rutgers University Press, 2002), 177.
4 Ibid.
5 George Yancy, *Reframing the Practice of Philosophy: Bodies of Color, Bodies of Knowledge* (Albany, NY: SUNY Press, 2012), 131.

of intellectual, moral and spiritual improvement, and to teach them the divine art and science of doing good to others."[1] Though originally prevented from being chartered due to abolitionist views,[2] the institution was soon given official state recognition and its first class of three graduated in 1863.[3] In the 20th century, the faculty and staff were encouraged to develop new and innovative methods for achieving the original goals,[4] which was the case when Catherine was hired. It was, in Paul Homan's words, "guided by the idea that the greater difficulty lies in learning how to 'include oneself in the world.'"[5]

Catherine said Olivet was a place "dedicated to learning," and "one where both students and faculty were dedicated toward learning without the constraints of accreditation and tenure."[6] She recalled it had a varied, international staff and curriculum.[7] The college had the Oxford tutorial system and attracted affluent students from across the nation.[8] She ranked her experience there with her later experience at North Dakota State University as the two high points in her teaching experience, relating them as putting no pressure on her and allowing her the freedom to choose what she did in the classroom; or, as she put it, "I get away with murder."[9] That would not be a permanent condition at Olivet.

Gertrude Stein and Robert Frost were among the poets who visited the college when she was there.[10] Catherine also noted, "The students were extraordinarily literate, though sometimes their fluency overcame their knowledge—glibness without substance."[11] In all, as Nancy Hanson described, it was an exciting atmosphere for the young, idealistic teacher. Students and teachers were unusually close, and spontaneous debates were

1 "Our History," Olivet College, http://www.olivetcollege.edu/content/our-history.
2 Ibid.
3 Ibid.
4 Ibid.
5 Homan, "A Humanist in Honors," 88.
6 Shenk, "All in the Name of Learning".
7 Ibid.
8 Hanson, "Catherine Cater," 22.
9 Vanorny, interview of Catherine Cater, Tape B.
10 Ibid, Tape A.
11 Hanson, "Catherine Cater," 22.

held day and night. The participants were intrigued by their experiment in education.[1] The tutorial approach and debate, with Catherine as the moderator, would be her method, and she became schooled in it at this small institution. By her second year, she received mention for having broken through the barriers and landed the job she so obviously should have had. The *Pittsburgh Courier*, a newspaper that appealed to an African-American audience, mentioned both Catherine and her husband in an article titled, "Steady Growth: 60 Race Teachers In White Colleges."[2]

Catherine recalls that she and her husband traveled together at this time, including going to Europe to study labor governments and going to visit London.[3] While she spoke of crossing on the Queen Mary or the Queen Elizabeth, she and Cornelius returned, sailing from Gothenburg, Sweden, aboard the *Gripsholm* on August 24, 1946, and arrived in New York on September 3.[4] Overseas voyages would become common for Catherine but this may have been a first for both. They were traveling on passports issued in June of that year, Catherine's being number 91954, and Cornelius' having been issued by the Department of State, which indicates he still had government ties in June, 1946.[5]

That wasn't all they did together. In her 2005 interview Catherine gives the impression that she made a choice and had an adventure on her own; it is her invisibility cloak speaking, as it was a couple's venture. Along with showing the secretiveness Catherine came to adopt, this also shows her commitment to helping the less fortunate. In that interview, she said she talked to a man who had written about the South and said she wanted to go to worst place that had some hope. Following his suggestion, she went to a segregated Mississippi school, Jackson State College. This account may be true, but it is incomplete. As was reported, again by the *Pittsburgh Courier*, both Catherine and her husband went there that summer. The *Courier* carried photos of

---

1 Ibid.
2 Albert Anderson, "Steady Growth: 60 Race Teachers In White Colleges," *Pittsburgh Courier*, Feb 1, 1947, 3.
3 Vanorny, interview of Catherine Cater, Tape B.
4 Records of the U.S. Customs Service, Passenger list, US Citizens aboard the *Gripsholm* sailing from Gothenburg Sweden, arriving in New York on August 24, 1946.
5 Ibid.

both of them and reported, "Among outstanding faculty person-nel of the Jackson College, Jackson, Miss., during the summer session are Dr. Cornelius L. Golightly, and his charming wife, Dr. Catherine Cater, both holding doctorates from the Univer-sity of Michigan. Over one thousand students are enrolled in the college."[1]

Baptist missionaries had founded Jackson State as a private school in 1877 to educate Mississippi's freed slaves. It had de-veloped into a two-year institution where educational activi-ties were mainly focused on in-service education for teachers. In 1934 it became a public school, and expanded to a full four-year curriculum in in 1942.[2] As to the situation they were tak-ing on, Mississippi was represented in the Senate by Theodore Bilbo, who wrote a book that was released the year Catherine and her husband arrived, with the title *Take Your Choice: Separa-tion or Amalgamation.*[3] He violently opposed integration and was sure it would lead to miscegenation, or interracial relations and mixed race children, mulattoes such as Catherine. His view of this was, "the writer of this book would rather see his race and his civilization blotted out with the atomic bomb than to see it slowly but surely destroyed in the maelstrom of miscegenation, interbreeding, intermarriage and mongrelization."[4]

As described in Vanorny's interview, Catherine arrived there in the summer and there was a faculty meeting, where the ad-ministration announced that salaries would be increased by a dollar per month. While many faculty members clapped, Cath-erine, who was on stage as a new faculty member, walked out. Like the little girl who wouldn't stand during the school assem-bly, she was again called in for her behavior.

She taught World Literature, and many of the students were sent to class by what she called "plantation owners."[5] Since her students worked in fall and spring, many only attended for three months of the year, which would have had little effect on her as a

---

1 "Guest Professors," *Pittsburgh Courier*, Aug 2, 1947, 22.
2 "JSU History," *Jackson State University*, http://www.jsums.edu/unite/jsu-history/.
3 Theodore G. Bilboe, *Take Your Choice: Separation or Amalgamation* (Poplarville, Miss: Dream House Pub. Co., 1946).
4 Ibid., Preface, first page of book but unnumbered.
5 Vanorny, interview of Catherine Cater, Tape A

summer school teacher. She carried on, using an anthology with which she was familiar, and gave her students readings. This was not very successful and one student, who had been designated as the group spokesman, said to her, "We don't understand a thing you're talking about or anything in this book."[1] The problem was a simple one—they could not read. Following that, she divided them into groups, and read to them outside, then explained the ideas using basic, elementary language; and they understood it.[2] She made the most of the situation and as always, found a way to bring the great ideas of Western culture to an inexperienced audience.

She recalled the great magnolia tree where mixed-race groups would rally and the inspirational singing that was enjoyed. One special man would sing and "hit" a crescendo that was especially memorable and enthralled the gathering.[3] This stay in the South was a swan song, though she would return for visits later.

Another thing she did at this time with her husband was to give a presentation on "Race Relations." This was for a class called "Current Social Problems."[4] For this, as for everything,[5] Catherine continued to use as her surname "Cater," which was a highly unusual choice to make in the 1940s. The shift among college-educated women to keeping their surname after marriage began sometime from the mid-1970s to the early 1980s.[6] Whether this was indicative of the state of their marriage or Catherine's nature and determination to not be someone's property is unknown.

In July of 1948, Catherine's "verse" attracted attention. She received a letter sent on July 27 from C.A. Pollard, of Doubleday & Company, Inc., about a poem of hers for a book being compiled by Arna Bontemps and Langston Hughes, to be called "Modern

---

1 Ibid.
2 Ibid.
3 Ibid.
4 *Michigan Christian Advocate* (Detroit: Michigan Christian Advocate Publishing Company, Vol. 75, 1948), xxxix.
5 Catherine put Golightly in parenthesis on the ship's records for the *Gripsholm* manifest, *National Archives and Records Administration*, Year: 1946; Arrival: New York.
6 Claudia Goldin and Maria Shim. "Making a Name: Women's Surnames at Marriage and Beyond," *The Journal of Economic Perspectives*, Vol. 18, No. 2, Spring 2004, 159.

Negro Poetry." The letter, addressed to "Miss Cater," named the poem and stated, "This letter is to ask permission to include this poem in all editions of our volume published throughout the world, in the English language."[1] The poem was "Here and Now," and it would appear not only when it was first released in 1951 in *The Poetry of the Negro*,[2] but in subsequent editions of *American Negro Poetry* in 1963, 1975, and 1995.[3]

Catherine Cater's "Here and Now":
>If here and now be but a timely span
>>Between today's unhappiness, tomorrow's
>Joys, what if today's abundant sorrows
>>Never end, tomorrow never comes, what then?
>If youth, impatient of the disrespect
>>Accorded it, yearns to be old,
>>Age chafes beneath the manifold
>Losses of its prime and mourns neglect;
>So let it be for here and now, my dear,
>>Not for the when of an eternity;
>>No gazer in the crystal ball can see
>The future as we see the now and here.[4]

Catherine and Husband as Olivet College professors in 1947 (photo credit: The Pittsburgh Courier)

---

1 Box 1, Folder 37, Letter, C.A. Pollard, to Catherine Cater, July 27, 1948, Catherine Cater Collection, North Dakota State University (NDSU) Institute for Regional Studies & Universities Archives, Fargo, ND

2 *The Poetry of the Negro* (Garden City, New York: Doubleday & Company, 1951),192.

3 Arna Bontemps, *American Negro Poetry*. New York: Hill and Wang, 1963, Arna Bontemps au/ed., *American Negro Poetry, Revised Edition*, New York: Hill and Wang, 1975, 140, "Then and Now" appeared in American Negro Poetry, au/ed. Arna Wendell Bontemps au/ed., St. Louis: Turtleback Books, 1995, 140.

4 *Poetry Explorer*, Classic and Contemporary Poetry, HERE AND NOW, by CATHERINE CATER, *http://www.poetryexplorer.net/poem. php?id=10047414.*

CHAPTER 7. RED SCARE AND UPHEAVAL, THE 1948–1949 SCHOOL YEAR

By the time Catherine was in her third year at Olivet, outside forces would enter into her life. It was the post-War world and some things had changed, while others remained constant and resisted change. There was a boom in college enrolment that seemed likely to benefit Caroline as far as future employment possibilities were concerned. President Roosevelt signed into law the Serviceman's Readjustment Act, commonly known as the G.I. Bill, on June 22, 1944,[1] providing unprecedented federal support for education to veterans of World War II. At the War's end returning veterans accounted for 70% of all male enrolment at America's colleges and universities.[2] The trend only increased in the years immediately following. College enrollments nearly doubled between the fall of 1945 and the fall of 1946 and by 1947 enrollment was 70% higher than the prewar level.[3]

The effect of the GI Bill on the class that began in 1948 was summarized at the school year's end as, "In June 1949 *Fortune*

---

1 John Bound and Sarah Turner, "Going to War and Going to College: Did World War II and the G.I. Bill Increase Educational Attainment for Returning Veterans?," *Journal of Labor Economics*, Vol. 20, No. 4, Oct 2002,790.
2 Ibid., 785
3 Marcus Stanley, "College Education and the Midcentury GI Bills," *The Quarterly Journal of Economics*, Vol. 118, No. 2, May 2003, 677.

published its findings of the class of 1949, 70 percent of whom were veterans, and reported: 'To most of those who have worked closely with it—from the professors and the placement directors to the recruiters for industry—'49 is the best class the country has ever produced.' Two years later *Time*, voicing a common opinion, classified the G.I. Bill as 'the most ambitious educational experiment in the nation's history."[1] These were the members of what journalist and author Tom Brokaw called "the greatest generation."[2]

There was a new sense of optimism following the War as America struggled to readjust and get back to normal. Joltin' Joe DiMaggio, America's sports hero of the time, his black hair flecked with gray, was back in the Yankee lineup after reporting for military service in 1943.[3] In America's pastime, things were changing as on April 15, 1947, Jackie Robinson broke the color barrier when he took the field for the Brooklyn Dodgers.[4] Families were being started in record numbers as a part of largest generation ever born in the U.S.,[5] the Baby Boomers that began following the end of World War II.[6] Catherine and Cornelius were not included in adding to that statistic.

Accompanying all of this was a growing fear that engulfed

---

1 Keith W. Olson, "The G. I. Bill and Higher Education: Success and Surprise," *American Quarterly*, Vol. 25. No. 5. Dec 1973, 596.

2 Tom Brokaw, *The Greatest Generation* (New York: Random House, 2001).

3 Baseball's Joe DiMaggio Dies at 84," *Los Angeles Times*, March 9, 1999.

4 Kenneth L. Shropshire, Associate Professor of Legal Studies at Wharton School, University of Pennsylvania, states "One could argue that Jackie Robinson coming to the plate on April 15, 1947 was the most visible, and therefore in some ways the most important, moment in recent American civil rights history." Kenneth L. Shropshire, "Where Have You Gone, Jackie Robinson?: Integration in America in the 21st Century," *South Texas Law Review*, Vol. 38, 1043.

5 Doug Owram, *Born at the Right Time: A History of the Baby Boom Generation*, (Toronto: University of Toronto Press), 98.

6 The U.S. Census Department defines Baby boomers as those born between mid- 1946 and mid 1964, Sandra L. Colby and Jennifer M. Ortman, "The Baby Boom Cohort in the United States: 2012 to 2060, Current Population Reports," May 2014, 2. This is the definition used by Donald J. Bogue, Douglas L. Anderton, Richard E. Barrett, *The Population of the United States: 3rd Edition* (New York: Simon& Schuster, Jul 2010), 403, and is common in other standard sources, and 76 million is a common figure used for the total number of Baby boomers.

---

everyone and would alter Catherine's idyllic ivory-tower life at Olivet. It had begun as World War II was drawing to an end. Shortly after the defeat of Germany and Japan, a competition had hardened into a new kind of struggle between the two surviving great powers, nuclear-armed America and the Soviet Union with its massive Red Army. The Soviets had laid claim to all territory they liberated from the Axis powers and established pro-Soviet governments to control them. Winston Churchill famously stated this in his address at Westminster College in Fulton, Missouri, on March 5, 1946, with President Truman sitting on the stage. After he expressed "strong admiration and regard for the valiant Russian people and my wartime comrade, Marshall Stalin," Churchill continued, "From Stettin in the Baltic to Trieste in the Adriatic, an iron curtain has descended across the Continent."[1] The Soviets hoped to export communism worldwide and in the U.S. there was concern about communist sympathizers who might assist them. President Truman issued the Loyalty order of March 21, 1947,[2] that required a check on the patriotic allegiance of all federal employees.[3] The House Un-American Activities Committee and the F.B.I. under J. Edgar Hoover, who was quick to equate protests of any kind with communist subversion, accompanied this new concern about loyalty with investigations.[4]

The Iron Curtain was the name for a dividing line and soon the conflict between the communists and "free" world received a name. Industrialist and financier Bernard Baruch called on an old friend, journalist Herbert Baynard Swope, for help in writing a speech he was to give in April 1947, in South Carolina. Swope came up with an effective phrase. Baruch delivered his speech and said, "Let us not be deceived—today we are in the midst

---

1 "Mr. Churchill's Address for United Effort for World Peace," *New York Times*, March 6, 1946, 4.

2 For an in depth discussion see Seth W. Richardson, and Harry S. Truman, "The Federal Employee Loyalty Program," *Columbia Law Review*, Vol. 51, No. 5, May 1951. See also Robert Justin Goldstein. "Prelude to McCarthyism: The Making of a Blacklist," National Archives, Vol. 38, No. 3, Fall 2006, http://www.archives.gov/publications/prologue/2006/fall/agloso.html.

3 "The Red Scare," *History*, http://www.history.com/topics/cold-war/red-scare.

4 Ibid.

of a cold war."[1] Popular syndicated columnist Walter Lippmann popularized the label[2] and the Cold War became the name of the conflict that would persist over the next 40 years.

The Cold War struck Catherine in the fall of 1948 when, as she recalled, she "woke up one day and there was this young man in class"[3] that she mistook for a parent of one of her students. She asked him which student, and, "He smiled blithely and pulled out his FBI badge."[4] She was under surveillance, as some students had apparently reported that the materials some of the professors at Olivet were using and some of their activities were un-American.[5] That included Catherine's innocuous comment that was deemed to be a communist idea—that not everyone who should go to college could go to college.[6] The FBI didn't take her comments or activities as anything dangerous,[7] but four of her colleagues were fired, including "a gentleman given to wearing walking shorts and carrying a walking stick, and with a goatee."[8]

Conor Shenk of North Dakota State University's weekly paper the *Spectrum* described this as "life-changing contact with the McCarthy 'Red Scare.' "[9] While "McCarthyism" didn't actually arrive until 1950, it was a precursor to his era. Catherine resigned effective at the end of the year in protest to "fight the good fight,"[10] along with her husband and a number of her other colleagues. There were student rallies in support of the faculty members who had been fired that included marchers from the University of Chicago, and Norman Thomas spoke in support at

---

1 Lawrence D. Freedman, "Frostbitten: Decoding the Cold War, 20 Years Later". *Foreign Affairs* Vol. 89, No.2, Mar/Apr 2010, 138.
2 Walter Lippmann, *The Cold War: A Study in U.S. Foreign Policy* (New York: Harper Brothers, 1947).
3 Conor Shenk, "All in the Name of Learning," *Spectrum* (North Dakota State University), Nov 3, 2000, 4, Folder 22, Catherine Cater Collection, North Dakota State University Institute for Regional Studies & Universities Archives, Fargo, ND.
4 Ibid.
5 Ibid.
6 Vanorny, interview of Catherine Cater, Tape A.
7 Ibid.
8 Hanson, "Catherine Cater," 22.
9 Shenk, "All in the Name of Learning," 4.
10 Vanorny, interview of Catherine Cater, Tape A.

a rally.[1] Thomas was a repeated Socialist Party nominee for the presidency.

As the year moved on there was a reminder of Catherine's past when the election of 1948 came around. It was a presidential election year when racial concerns took on considerable importance. The Black vote was seen as a critical factor, since Truman was running for election on his own after coming to office on the death of Franklin Roosevelt. The previous year, special counsel to the President Clark Clifford had prepared a memo for Truman that warned, "Unless there are new and real efforts, the Negro bloc...will go Republican."[2] He contended, "It is inconceivable that any policies initiated by the Truman administration, no matter how 'liberal,' could so alienate the South in the next year that it would revolt."[3] The "solid South" had voted Democrat since the election of Lincoln in 1860 divided the country. In the Cold War, American racism was a useful propaganda tool for its Soviet rival to exploit in Africa and Asia.[4]

On February 2, 1948, Truman sent Congress his special committee's report, *To Secure These Rights*,[5] and asked for its recommendations to be enacted as laws. He requested that the "Do-Nothing Congress" make lynching a federal crime, abolish the poll tax, end discrimination in employment, segregation on interstate transportation and establish a civil rights division in the Justice Department.[6] His hope was to walk a fine line with politicians from the South but their reaction was outrage.

During a hot summer, Philadelphia hosted the Republicans' and Democrats' nomination conventions and also the Progressive Party of former vice president Henry Wallace. Both the major parties chose Philadelphia because it was the mid-point

---

1 Hanson, "Catherine Cater," 28.

2 Confidential memorandum to President, November 19, 1947, Clark M. Clifford Papers, cited in Harvard Sitkoff, "Harry Truman and the Election of 1948: The Coming of Age of Civil Rights in American Politics," *The Journal of Southern History*, Vol. 27, No. 4, Nov 1971, 597.

3 Clifford memorandum quoted in Sean J. Savage, "To Purge or Not to Purge: Hamlet Harry and the Dixiecrats, "1948-1952, *Presidential Studies Quarterly*, Vol. 27, No. 4, Fall 1997.

4 Sitkoff, "Harry Truman and the Election of 1948, 597-597.

5 *To Secure These Rights*, Harry S Truman Library and Museum, access online at www.blackpast.org/african-american-history-primary-documents.

6 Ibid., 600-601.

on the coaxial cable from Boston to Richmond. For the first time ever, the conventions were going to be televised. Edward R. Murrow and others whose voices were familiar radio presences would be visible to primarily an East Coast public.[1] It is very likely Catherine and Cornelius followed this on the radio, as television coverage did not extend to small town Wisconsin.

The Republicans were optimistic after four losses to Franklin Roosevelt when they began on June 21. Their front-runner was Thomas Dewey, but three days after the convention began the Cold War grew tense as the Soviet Union launched a blockade of West Berlin, cutting off all ground transportation to the free half of Berlin that sat isolated in Communist East Germany. Many of the convention speeches were about Communism, Truman's weakness in dealing with the Communists, and Communist infiltration of the government and college campuses; this came not long after the investigations into Olivet College.[2] Dewey received the Republican nomination and his running mate was Earl Warren of California. They included a civil rights statement that "Lynching or any other form of mob violence is a disgrace to any civilized state and we favor prompt enactment of legislation to end this infamy," opposition to a poll tax for voting, and an end of segregation in the armed forces of the United States.[3]

Two weeks after the Republicans departed, the Democrats arrived and in their party platform, they hoped to accommodate two important constituencies, Blacks and White Southerners. Liberals feared that Wallace and his Progressive Party would win the Black vote from the Democrats.[4] They wanted the items Truman had identified in his civil rights message to Congress, including abolition of state poll taxes in federal elections, an anti-lynching law, fair employment practices and desegregation of the armed forces. Minneapolis Mayor Hubert Humphrey "won

1 Alonzo L. Hamby, "1948 Democratic Convention: The South Secedes Again," *Smithsonian Magazine*, Aug 2008, www.smithsonianmag.com/.../1948-democratic-convention-11
2 "GOP Convention of 1948 in Philadelphia," www.ushistory.org/gop/convention_1948...
3 Ibid.
4 Sitkoff, "Harry Truman and the Election of 1948, 608.

loud cheers and boos"[1] as he presented the demands, saying, "The time is now arrived in America for the Democratic Party to get out of the shadow of states' rights and walk forthrightly into the bright sunshine of human rights."[2] When civil rights measures were included and a states' rights provision was voted down, half of Alabama's and all of Mississippi's delegates, a total of 35, walked out of the convention in protest.[3]

Truman, in accepting his nomination, challenged the Republicans to stand up for what they had written into their platform and announced he was calling Congress back into session, saying, "If there is any reality behind that Republican platform, we ought to get some action from a short session of the 80th Congress. They can do this job in 15 days, if they want to do it. They will still have time to go out and run for office."[4]

Two days after the Democratic Convention, 6,000 individuals from thirteen Southern states met in a Birmingham, Alabama hall singing "Dixie" and waving Confederate flags;[5] they nominated Governor Strom Thurmond of South Carolina for President and Governor Fielding Wight of Mississippi for Vice President on the States Rights Party, or as they were called, the "Dixicrats." Their platform consisted of condemning the civil rights statement in the Democratic Party platform and insisting on segregation of Blacks and asserting states' rights.[6]

The Congress met and Truman gave a speech calling for action on civil rights. The Republican Party's national chairman and the chairman of the Senate Foreign Relations Committee Robert Taft said, "No, we're not going to give that fellow anything,"[7] and blocked all legislation proposed. It gave Truman more to campaign on against on the "Do-Nothing Congress" where the Republicans controlled both the House of Represen-

---

1 W.H. Lawrence, "Truman, Barkley Named by Democrats; South Loses on Civil Rights, 35 Walk Out; President Will Recall Congress July 26," *New York Times*, July 15, 1948.
2 Hamby, "1948 Democratic Convention".
3 Lawrence, "Truman, Barkley Named by Democrats"
4 "Truman's Democratic Convention Acceptance Speech: July 15, 1948," www.pbs.org/newshour/spc/character/links/truman_speech.html.
5 Robert H. Ferrell, "The Last Hurrah," *The Wilson Quarterly*, Vol. 12, No. 2, Spring 1988, 71.
6 Boorstin and Kelley, *A History of the United States*, 609.
7 Ferrell, "The Last Hurrah," 73.

tatives and the Senate. Truman acted on his own and on July 28, 1948, issued Executive Order 9981, abolishing racial segregation in the armed forces of the United States.[1]

When November came, Harry Truman was elected President in a shock outcome. The polls all had Dewey anywhere from five to 15 points ahead, so when the election came out with Truman winning by 4.4%,[2] it caught many off guard. That including the *Chicago Tribune*, which had called the president a "nincompoop"[3] on its editorial page and printed the banner headline "DEWEY DEFEATS TRUMAN" for its November 2 run before waiting for the results to come in. Strom Thurmond's Dixicrat Party received the second most popular votes; edging the Republicans by 39.7% to 35.6%[4] The South remained alive and well.

But the South was not where Catherine wanted to go, having quit her job. There had been other drama that year. Her marriage, which had perhaps never been strong, had disintegrated. Whether she was hurt or bore resentment would never be known, for if she did, she buried it deep inside. Her husband's biography reports, "Cold War restrictions on the faculty's academic freedom prompted Golightly and his spouse, Catherine Cater, to leave Olivet College in protest in 1949."[5] What that biography fails to note is that when they left, they headed in different directions. No evidence of what led to the breakup presents itself, and on paper the couple appeared well matched, both highly educated and respected. What went on in their marriage is lost, and if it offers any hint, he appears to have moved on easily. Though their divorce would not be final until the following year, in 1950,[6] he wasted little time in making news in the African-American community. *Jet* magazine of January 10, 1952,

---

1 "Executive Order 9981: Desegregation of the Armed Forces (1948)," www.ourdocuments.gov/doc.php?doc=84.
2 Bonnie K. Goodman, "1948: Presidential Campaign & Elections," https://presidentialcampaignselectionsreference.wordpress.com/ overviews/20th-century/1948-overview/.
3 Reneé Critcher Lyons, "The Second Shall Be First: 1948 Presidential Election – Truman V. Dewey, *Our White House: Looking In, Looking Out*, http://www.ourwhitehouse.org/secondshallbefirst.html.
4 Lyons, "The Second Shall Be First".
5 "Dr. Cornelius Golightly (1917-1976): The Life of an Academic and Public Intellectual".
6 *Finding Aid to the Catherine Cater Papers*, "Biography," 3.

---

carried the story "Negro Teacher Weds White Coed," in which he was described as "handsome" and "brilliant" and added, "His first wife was Dr. Catherine Cater, daughter of Talladega College's Dean James Tate Cater."[1]

Following his departure from Olivet at the end of the 1949 school year, Cornelius Golightly was "quickly hired by the Philosophy Department at the University of Wisconsin at Madison,"[2] while, in what Catherine described as her "most dramatic experience,"[3] she and a group of six of her colleagues decided to head off and try to found a college of their own. The now liberated Catherine and her friends all had debts, and "We all got in this beat-up car and rode to Sackets Harbor, New York."[4] On the way they wrote up a curriculum,[5] and they obtained a former army barracks from the federal government as a campus.[6] It was a short-lived effort. They had support from parents and students, but no money, and could not "make the state charter for the college to start up."[7] Unlike her employed, estranged husband, Catherine was desperate for work with the fall of 1949 approaching.

---

1 "Negro Teacher Weds White Coed," *Jet*, Jan 10, 1952, 15.
2 Ibid.
3 Kosse, "Cater: 'infect one another with the desire to learn' ".
4 Shenk, "All in the Name of Learning," 4.
5 Vanorny, interview of Catherine Cater, Tape A.
6 Homan, "A Humanist in Honors," 88.
7 Shenk, "All in the Name of Learning," 4.

CHAPTER 8. NO WOMEN WANTED, MINNESOTA OPPORTUNITY IN A CHANGING AMERICA

The 1949 school year was approaching and an anxious Catherine was down to her "last black dress."[1] She went to the placement office at the University of Michigan seeking a last minute opening. A placement officer at the University said of the African-American woman he saw before him, "You're like a person without legs or arms. I can't place you anywhere."[2]

She sent out many letters, all with addresses in the North,[3] but continuously received negative responses. One Minnesota college wrote, "We are not yet ready for women."[4] Eventually she did receive one possibility for a position, when Dr. O. W. Snarr, the president of Moorhead State Teachers College in Moorhead, Minnesota, replied to her. A member of Snarr's faculty, English professor Clarence "Soc" Glasrud, had obtained a leave to attend Harvard[5] and Snarr needed to find a replacement. Catherine had previously met Glasrud when she was teaching at Olivet and attended a summer session on literary criticism at Kenyon College in Ohio.[6]

1 Vanorny, interview of Catherine Cater, Tape A.
2 Ibid.
3 Homan, "A Humanist in Honors," 88.
4 Vanorny, interview of Catherine Cater, Tape A.
5 Hanson, "Catherine Cater," 24.
6 Ibid.

She arranged to meet with Dr. Snarr for an interview at the Stevens Hotel in Chicago, and wearing her only black dress, she brought her father along to the interview.[1] Having her father accompany her and meet Snarr was probably a wise move. Perhaps Catherine knew of Snarr's background and academic training. Snarr was born in West Virginia in 1886,[2] three years before Catherine's father was born in Georgia, and he received his master's degree and PhD from the University of Chicago.[3] This would have exposed him to many of the ideas on education that inspired Catherine's father, and that he instituted at Talladega and passed on to his daughter. The interview was a success and Catherine was offered a one-year replacement position that came with responsibilities as a librarian,[4] along with English Department duties. She observed, "That's how I came [to Fargo-Moorhead]. They needed someone to fill in while he [Glasrud] was gone. I never knew in those days how long I'd be here. Clarence just kept staying and staying."[5]

Catherine moved to Fargo-Moorhead in the fall of 1949, not realizing she had found her permanent home. Moorhead, Minnesota, and Fargo, North Dakota, are one metropolitan area that at the time included a population of 89,340.[6] The north running Red River divides the two cities and the two states. For the 66 years until her death it was where she would remain.

It was also the time at which she made a defining choice that must be noted. Up to this point she had lived her life as an African-American and her experiences, from childhood, had been of being defined as such, beginning from her early memory of hiding under a bed from the Ku Klux Klan as it marched through the

1 Ibid, Vanorny, interview of Catherine Cater, Tape A.
2 "Biographical Note," Snarr, Otto Welton, 1886–1966. Collection, 1857–1968, Minnesota State University, Mankato, Memorial Library, Southern Minnesota Historical Center Snarr, Otto Welton, 1886–1966. Collection, 1857–1968.
3 Ibid.
4 Homan, "A Humanist in Honors," 88.
5 Hanson, "Catherine Cater," 24.
6 Howard G. Brunsman, supervisor, "Population of Standard Metropolitan Statistical Areas and Component Areas in the United States and the Commonwealth of Puerto Rico: 1940–1960," *The Eighteenth Decennial Census of the United States, Census of Population: Volume I, Characteristics of the Population, Part A, Number of Inhabitants* (U.S. Department of Commerce, Bureau of the Census) 1-101.

Talladega campus in Alabama. She had led her college chapter of the NAACP, and her career success had been reported in a paper for the African-American community, the *Pittsburgh Courier*. Catherine's poetry was published in the original and subsequent editions of *American Negro Poetry*. Her still husband, though estranged at the time of arriving in Fargo-Moorhead, would be a noted leader in the Black community, as the first African-American elected to the school board of the Milwaukee public schools[1] and first Black president of the Detroit School Board,[2] as well as a leading intellectual. At that time, the estimated population of people of African descent in United States and Canada, partly or entirely, was 14,916,000, which was second in the Americas to Brazil's 17,529,000, though the numbers "must be taken as extremely imprecise at best" as the determination was often at the whim of census taker.[3]

Upon arriving in Fargo-Moorhead Catherine no longer identified herself as an African-American. This was clearly a conscious choice. While it would always raise uncertainties, they seemed indelicate and were not directly addressed, as they would appear unimportant, and to question her could have been insulting once she became established. Her close friend Mike Morrissey said, "She certainly could have easily passed for white if she had wanted to."[4] Yvonne Condell, an African-American who was named to *Who's Who in America in 1965*,[5] had understandable questions. Yvonne and her husband James played very important roles in Moorhead State University's history. She was a Georgia native who grew up in Florida and did her undergraduate work at Florida University, then earned her masters and PhD in biology from the University of Connecticut.[6] She and her husband

1 "Golightly, Cornelius L., 1917–1976: Biography, Civil Rights Digital Library: Documenting America's Struggle for Racial Equality, http://crdl.usg.edu/people/g/golightly_cornelius_l_1917_1976/?Welcome.
2 "Dr. Cornelius Golightly (1917-1976): The Life of an Academic and Public Intellectual".
3 Philip D. Curtin, *The Atlantic Slave Trade: A Census* (Madison, Madison, WI: University of Wisconsin Press, 1972), 91.
4 Mike Morrissey interview with Robert Dodge, Oct 9, 2015, Fargo, ND.
5 "1960s Timeline," University Archives, Minnesota State University Moorhead, https://www.mnstate.edu/university-archives/125th-anniversary/1960s/.
6 Yvonne Condell, interview with Robert Dodge, October 9, 2015.

Jim had been working at Florida A and M in Tallahassee where he was a clinical psychologist and they ended up in the Midwest because he heard of an interesting program at the University of North Dakota. They took a leave of absence and left and Jim was offered position at Jamestown, the home of the North Dakota State Hospital for the mentally ill, to train people to be clinical psychologists in an effort to make their treatment community based. When their two-year leave ran out, they had to decide whether to return to Florida A and M. They chose to resign, taking jobs in Minnesota at Fergus Falls, where Jim worked at the Hospital for the Mentally Ill in the facility for children with Down's Syndrome and mental retardation, and Yvonne taught at the community college.[1]

They were the first African-Americans in Fergus Falls, a community of 12,000, and were accepted and able to make friends. Jim was one of eight psychologists on staff and invited to be a Rotarian, since "movers and shakers were Rotarians."[2] He was also an outstanding musician and his guitar performances would become well known throughout the area, including having him invited back as featured soloist with the Fergus Fall civic orchestra after their departure.[3]

An unfortunate first encounter with Catherine soured their relationship that will soon be addressed, but while the Condells were working in Fergus Falls, Dr. John Neumaier had become president of Moorhead State. When he learned of the couple with PhDs working in Fergus Falls, he recruited them to come to teach at Moorhead State. That was in 1965, after Catherine had already left the institution.

When they arrived, people said to Yvonne, "Jim and I were the first African-American faculty members at M.S. (Moorhead State)."[4] She had already had an encounter with Catherine by this time and she responded with, "Are we? I left it at that, because I didn't want to say that Catherine was here. So, if you ask somebody, 'Who were the first African-American faculty mem-

1 Ibid.
2 Ibid.
3 "Fergus Falls Civic Orchestra Spring Concert: Soloist – James Condell," *Daily Journal* (Fergus Falls, MN), Apr 6, 1973, 5.
4 Yvonne Condell, interview with Robert Dodge.

bers at M.S,' they'll say, 'The Condells.' "[1] She added that when the Condells came to Moorhead in 1965, there was only one African-American living there, and he was at the Army induction center in Fargo. "We were African-Americans two and three,"[2] since Catherine had moved across the river to Fargo.

This is a part of her rationale for not sharing the commonly held high regard for Catherine, and from her perspective it is understandable. Fargo-Moorhead in the 1960s was very lacking in racial diversity and for the trailblazers like the Condells, who eventually established a scholarship at Moorhead State for African-American students,[3] they arrived to find that Catherine seemed to be denying her heritage. It is not unreasonable that they would have appreciated having Catherine, who was an established leading intellectual in the community, declare herself to be an African-American and proud of her ethnicity.

Catherine's decision came before the Condells arrival, and I believe it is convincingly looked at in a different manner. She had lived in a world where she had been defined by race, but her classification by the census bureau had been "mulatto," so racially she was mixed. In 2005 she said, "I don't know what race I am, I'm so mixed up. It doesn't have too much meaning to me one way or another."[4] Her colleague at the North Dakota State University English Department, Steve Ward, said, "She thought there was some Indian blood there somewhere, but never indicated who it was. Cherokee maybe. Trail of tears, that sort of thing."[5] This is likely some story she heard in her childhood. The nineteen-volume *History from Slave Sources*[6] that was begun by Fisk University in the 1920s and completed by the Federal Writers Project of 1936–1938, then bound and published by the Library of Congress, says this was a common claim. According to their comprehensive interviews, "The number of ex-slaves

---

1 Ibid.
2 Ibid.
3 25 Great Scholarships for African American Students: MSU Moorhead James & Yvonne Condell Endowed Scholarship, http://www.top10on-linecolleges.org/scholarships-for/african-american-students/.
4 Vanorny, interview of Catherine Cater, Tape A.
5 Steve Ward interview with Robert Dodge, Oct 11, 2015, Fargo ND.
6 George P. Rawick, ed., *The American Slave: A Composite Autobiography* (Westport, Conn.: Greenwood Press, 1972).

who claimed Indian blood was remarkable. One Arkansas interviewer went so far as to say he 'never talked to a Negro who did not claim to be part Indian.' This was more prevalent in the Southwest than the Southeast, but also thought to be due to psychological reasons as having Indian blood was frequently invoked for having cherished traits including rebelliousness, fortitude and ferocity."[1]

Catherine's African-American origins had been imposed on her from the days of her Alabama youth and the times in which she grew up. She was not "passing" by not choosing to identify herself as African-American when she came to Fargo-Moorhead. To say that was the case would amount to accepting the eugenics definition of race, identifying a person as Black if that person had any African "blood." The "one drop rule" of Georgia and Alabama, where Catherine's ancestors and Catherine grew up, would say that she was African-American. That eugenic thinking still existed in the 1940s is seen in the case of *The Estate of Bradford Monks*,[2] which involved competing wills left by a wealthy Boston man, the first made out to a friend and the second to a woman he married late in life. In the probate trial, the judge heard testimony including a hairdressers' description of size of the moons of the wife's fingernails, and a Southern Baptist missionary who had once practiced in Africa and claimed that by walking near the woman, he could ascertain she was at least "1/8th negro blood" from the contour of her calves and heels. On this basis, the judge rule definitively that the wife was 7/8 Caucasian and 1/8 Negro, making the marriage invalid as a violation of the state's anti-miscegenation laws that prevented interracial marriage, so the wife's will was invalid.[3]

Leading scholars were challenging eugenics by the time Catherine arrived in Fargo-Moorhead in the later 1940s, and she was of a very mixed ancestry that did not pigeonhole her. Her heritage was not anymore African-American than non African-American, even though the White forefathers had abandoned responsibility. Up to this point she had been defined by race and

1 Woodward, "Review: History from Slave Sources," 480.
2 Estate of Allan Bradford Monks, Deceased. Ida Nancy Lee et al. v. Antoinette Giraudo, Civ. No. 2832. Fourth Dist, Dec, 19, 1941.
3 Pascoe, *What Comes Naturally*, 126-128.

had been successful, a "credit to her race." She had decided to no longer impose a definition of herself on others as African-American that was no more accurate than it was false.

While the culture may still like things simple, this was a time when in the world of popular anthropologists like Ashley Montagu and Gunnar Myrdal, racial classifications were being challenged as having no meaning. Catherine was following their lead, in that while she was not denying her racial heritage and proclaiming to be something else, she was just rejecting it as her definition. Others could have chosen to define Catherine racially when she arrived and she no doubt would have admitted her unspecific background, but since she made no issue of it one way or the other, it never became of any importance.

Leaving Michigan, she had decided to no longer be categorized, though she would support the civil rights movement that was emerging as well as the women's movement that would arise. She was not an activist in these movements and became more focused on generalized rights at a philosophical level, which drew her to the American Civil Liberty Union. She became the Catherine so many of us knew. She was Catherine, the person not of causes but of ideas. As Paul Homan explained, "There's a difference between being out there in the political forefront and just talking about it. I don't mean that activism was her thing, but the free exchange of information."[1]

When Catherine began work at Moorhead, the fear of communism that had led to her quitting her job at Olivet was heating up, as the situation in the world grew much more hazardous. That fear was taken seriously by some and exploited by others. President Truman had adopted the policy of containment in 1947, to confine communism to areas it had already captured and prevent it from gaining anything new. The U.S. had responded to Soviet threats of expansion by establishing the Marshall plan to revive the war torn economies of Europe in 1948 and joining the alliance, NATO, early in the following year. Events of 1949 at the time Catherine moved to Fargo-Moorhead shattered American confidence as few have in history. On the morning of September

---

1 Paul Homan interview.

23, President Truman summoned reporters, and his press secretary Charles Ross said, "Nobody is leaving until everybody has this statement."[1] Ross then handed out mimeographed sheets that stated, "We have evidence that within recent weeks an atomic explosion occurred within the U.S.S.R."[2] Banner headlines followed the next day and America's monopoly on nuclear weapons, which was its military advantage, had vanished. The world had become a much more dangerous place.

Very shortly after, on October 1, Mao Zedong declared the creation of the People's Republic of China,[3] and one-fifth of the world's population had been added to the ranks of communism,[4] after a civil war between the Chinese Communist Party and the Nationalist Party, or Kuomintang, which had governed China since the revolution of 1911 ended dynastic rule. The corrupt government of Nationalist leader Chiang Kai-Shek had cooperated with the Communist army during World War II but lacked popular support. It was driven out and established itself on the island of Taiwan, and the communist world was much larger.

America's increased fears about safety were highlighted in an ongoing debate among scientists. The United States had succeeded in building the atom bomb and the Soviets had recently exploded a fission bomb, a device that released a great amount of energy by the splitting of atoms. The possibility scientists had discovered when developing the fission bomb was to produce a fusion weapon, one that released energy by forcing the hydrogen atoms together. Nuclear fusion is the power by which the sun generates heat and light, and a weapon harnessing this energy might be hundreds or thousands of times as powerful as the atom bomb. Such a weapon was known to as the "superbomb," commonly referred to as the "super."

The dispute on whether to go ahead with development of the "super" had centered around two of America's leading, but dis-

---

1 Eric F. Goldman, *The Crucial Decade – And After: America, 1945-1960* (New York: Alfred A. Knopf, 1960), 99.
2 Ibid.
3 "The Chinese Revolution of 1949," *Department of State, Office of the Historian*, https://history.state.gov/milestones/1945-1952/chinese-rev.
4 There were 555, 000,000 Mainland Chinese in a world that totaled 2,556,000,000.

similar, nuclear physicists, J. Robert Oppenheimer and Edward Teller.[1] Oppenheimer had been director of the Manhattan Project that had developed the first atom bomb. He was opposed to going ahead with the new bomb. The dapper, Harvard educated scholar had ethical and practical reservations about development of the new fusion bomb. "I am not sure the miserable thing will work, nor that it can be gotten to target except by oxcart,"[2] said Oppenheimer, summarizing his technical opposition, though his moral opposition was that it would be the creation of a weapon of mass genocide.[3] He contended that atomic weapons already developed would be adequate as America's defense force against the Soviet Union. Teller was Oppenheimer's opposite in many ways. With his bushy eyebrows and rumpled suits, he walked with a limp on his prosthetic foot from an accident involving a trolley car when he was young.[4] Hungarian born, he had fled to the United States to escape the Nazi persecution of Jews in the 1930s. Also a veteran of the Manhattan project, Teller was convinced of the workability of a fusion bomb, and believed that if the U.S. did not develop it, the Soviets would, and that would be disastrous. There were leading nuclear scientists on both sides of the debate.[5]

The year 1949 came to a close with the nation's attention on the trial of Alger Hiss, a Harvard Law School graduate who had clerked for Supreme Court Justice Oliver Wendell Holmes and joined the State Department under President Roosevelt. At the urging of Representative Richard Nixon of California, he had been charged by the House Un-American Activities Commission

---

1 See Ashutosh Jogalekar, The Many Tragedies of Edward Teller, *Scientific American*, blogs.scientificamerican.com/.../the-many-tragedies-o..., Jan 15, 2014.
2 Editors of Time-Life Books, *This Fabulous Century 1950-1960*, Vol. VI (New York: Time-Life Books, 1972), 27.
3 Hydrogen Bomb – 1950," *Atomic Heritage Foundation*, www.atomicheritage.org/.../hydrogen-bomb...
4 "Edward Teller (1908–2003)," atomicarchive.com, www.atomicarchive.com › Library › Biographies.
5 See "Hydrogen Bomb — 1950," *Atomic Heritage Foundation*..berree Speech in the Age of McCf the U.S. is now intimidated."Catherine'ted party line with all Democrats voting i

as being a Soviet spy.[1] As 1950 began Alger Hiss was convicted for his involvement with the communist Whittaker Chambers.

The Alger Hiss decision instantly resolved the debate between Oppenheimer and Teller, not by scientists but by national security and insecurity. President Truman announced the U.S. was going ahead with development of the "super," or hydrogen bomb. Four days later a British physicist confessed to passing atomic secrets to the Soviets and his confession led to the arrest of other alleged conspirators, including Julius and Ethel Rosenberg in the U.S.[2] On February 12 the man who understood the secrets of the atom best went on television, with hair uncombed and wearing a sweater, to explain what Truman's decision to build the hydrogen bomb meant. Albert Einstein emerged from the ivory tower to say, "radioactive poisoning of the earth's atmosphere and hence annihilation of any life on earth has been brought within the range of technical possibilities . . . General annihilation beckons."[3] The Thermonuclear Age was about to begin.

The Cold War heated up when summer came. Saturday, June 24, President Truman was at home in Independence, Missouri, when the phone rang. Secretary of State Dean Acheson said, "Mr. President I have very serious news. The North Koreans have invaded South Korea."[4]

The Red Scare fear that brought surveillance to Catherine's classroom at Olivet was to be exploited in a great witch-hunt that began with a speech following the events of 1949, as real concerns about communism were growing into paranoia. What would ignite things was when the junior senator from Wisconsin, Joseph McCarthy, spoke to the Women's Republican Club in Wheeling, West Virginia, for their Lincoln's Birthday Address on February 9, 1950.[5] In that oft-discussed speech McCarthy is reported to have said, "In my opinion the State Department . . . is

---

1 John Ehrman, "A Half-Century of Controversy: The Alger Hiss Case," *Central Intelligence Agency*, https://www.cia.gov/library/center-for-the-study-of-intelligence/kent-csi/vol44no5/html/v44i5a01p.htm.
2 Geoffrey R. Stone, "Free Speech in the Age of McCarthy: A Cautionary Tale," *California Law Review*, Vol. 93, No. 5, Oct 2005, 1394.
3 Goldman, *The Crucial Decade — And After: America*, 137.
4 Harry S. Truman, "In Korean Crisis," *Life*, Feb 6, 1956, 127.
5 Goldman, *The Crucial Decade*, 142.

thoroughly infested with communists." He continued, "I hold in my hand a list of 205 names . . . known to the Secretary of State as members of the Communist Party."[1]

McCarthy had no list, and when asked by a reporter to produce it he said he had left it in another suit pocket,[2] and a Senate committee, the Tydings Committee, was appointed to look into McCarthy's charges. While the committee was doing its investigating McCarthy attacked, and said that the "egg-sucking phony Liberals" and their "pitiful squealing . . . would hold sacrosanct those Communists and queers" who had sold China into "atheistic slavery."[3] The committee findings were that his accusations represented "perhaps the most nefarious campaign of half-truth and untruth in the history of this republic."[4] That did nothing to stop the movement that was in its infancy. When the report was sent to the full Senate three times, all 96 senators voted party line, with all Democrats voting in favor and all Republicans voting against accepting its conclusions.[5] With Republican backing, McCarthy argued this was only evidence of traitors' infiltration of the government.[6]

Washington Post cartoonist Herb Block drew a cartoon on March 29, 1950 that showed the Chairman of Republican National Committee Guy Gabrielson, Senator Robert Taft, and several other leading Republican senators pushing a confused Republican elephant toward a stack of buckets of tar. The barrel on the top of the stack was especially large. On this largest barrel was the label "McCarthyism,"[7] and a new word entered had the language.[8] The witch hunts, revival of HUAC, black lists, book banning and stifling of free speech without fear of repercussion soon followed. A person who had been influential on Catherine,

---

1 Ibid.
2 Stone, "Free Speech in the Age of McCarthy," 1395.
3 Ibid.
4 Larry Blomstedt, *Truman, Congress, and Korea: The Politics of America's First Undeclared War* (Lexington, KY: University Press of Kentucky, 2016), 65.
5 Ibid., 66.
6 Stone, "Free Speech in the Age of McCarthy," 1395.
7 Goldman, *The Crucial Decade*, 145.
8 Samuel Walker, *Presidents and Civil Liberties from Wilson to Obama: A Story of Poor Custodians* (New York: Cambridge University Press, 2012), 139; Julian Zelizer, *Arsenal of Democracy* (Sydney, Aus: ReadHowYouWant. com, 2010) 166-167.

famous educator Robert Hutchins, said, "The entire teaching profession of the U.S. is now intimidated."[1]

McCarthyism would see Catherine become involved in an organization that was appropriate for her new identity and her personal view of issues. Where she had once had a cause, the NAACP, she would elevate that to a broader struggle and rather than a cause, fight for ideas. She would always be a champion of the free exchange of ideas, and the American Civil Liberties Union, or ACLU, became an important organization in her life and she became important in the organization. With the ACLU she could fight for rights of individual belief and self-expression, in the face of forces that were attempting to suppress all conflicting points of view. As a person whose life was governed by ideas and the free exchange of points of view, her classes would resonate with Socratic dialogue more and more once she established herself in Fargo-Moorhead. The ACLU would be her major platform for addressing issues to a wider public.

McCarthyism hit the campuses of Fargo-Moorhead. At North Dakota State University four professors were fired because of the Red Scare of the McCarthy era.[2] Catherine and I discussed this on May 5, 2012, and she named the people that she remembered who had been affected. I told her about Daniel Posin, who had been a big favorite of mine when I was in elementary school and he was Dr. Dan the Weatherman on the local WDAY TV, where he also had a science show that fascinated me. He would talk about the possibilities of life on other planets and draw stick figures of what they would have to look life, with huge torsos to hold large lungs for atmospheres with little oxygen. On other days he would give simple explanations of the theory of relativity, also accompanied with his doodles on chalkboards. While I thought his primary job was to be the weatherman, he had a PhD in physics from Berkeley, and before coming to Fargo he had been president of the National Academy of Sciences and had worked at the Radiation and Research Lab

---

1 Geoffrey R. Stone, "Free Speech in the Age of McCarthy: A Cautionary Tale," *California Law Review*, Vol. 93, No. 5, Oct., 2005, 1400.

2 John Biemer, "Daniel Q. Posin, 93," Chicago *Tribune*, May 26, 2003, http://articles.chicagotribune.com/2003-05-26/news/0305260108_1_depaul-university-university-professor-physics.

at MIT. After being expelled from NDSU during the McCarthy Era for his "dangerous beliefs" he would eventually be a six-time Emmy Award winner, as well as a six-time nominee for the Nobel Peace Prize.[1] It had been a thrill for me when he showed up at our house one evening and I saw my TV hero in person, as he had a very surreptitious conversation with my father. Following that he was no longer the weatherman and his science show was no longer on WDAY television. I did not understand what was happening at the time, but it became clear in later years. Catherine remembered him well and recalled his unfortunate expulsion that reduced the intellectual vitality of the community.

During her first year at Moorhead State she worked at the library and taught English, and also children's literature, filling in for Delsie Holmquist, who was on another assignment. When Glasrud did not return from his leave of absence the following year, she became a fulltime English instructor. She explains her changing role on the faculty as, "I worked under Professor Holmquist when she became dean of General Studies. I found that 'general studies' was exactly my cup of tea. My interests lie outside the realm of academic disciplines, little pillboxes into which knowledge is fitted. My concern lies with questions that need to be answered, which can't be tackled through any one discipline but which can be approached through many. I have wanted students to understand that the little boxes we call 'disciplines' are a convenience for the colleges, not a view of the world condition. It is entirely possible to know everything there is to know in one area without knowing how that small segment reflects life both within and without."[2] Together with Holmquist she experimented with the general education curriculum to develop "a chance to be creative with courses in critical thought, anthropology, and philosophy."[3]

Catherine quickly became established as an important figure in the Fargo-Moorhead community. When the North Dakota Federation of Business and Professional Women held a convention at Gardner Hotel in Fargo in the spring of 1951, Catherine was one of the two main speakers, along with Clarke Bassett,

1 Ibid.
2 Hanson, "Catherine Cater," 24.
3 Homan, "A Humanist in Honors," 89.

the President of Merchants National Bank and Trust of Fargo.[1] She had also begun traveling by this time, which would become a big part of her life. She went to Hawaii in the summer of 1951 and was on the manifest for Northwest Flight 702 from Honolulu for September 15, 1951.[2] The plane received a stamp from the Immigration and Naturalization Service at 3:16 p.m. on September 16 in Portland, Oregon.[3] There were two others among the 23 passengers, Agnes Huntley and Ann Hartje, who were listed as being born in North Dakota.[4] Whether this indicates Catherine was traveling with them is uncertain.

Delsie Holmquist described one of Catherine's defining contributions to Moorhead State: "When she first came there was a group of insurgent students, we had them even then. Some of [the faculty] found them annoying and disruptive. Miss Cater brought them together in a group called Concentrics. Here they talked, discussed, condemned, but somehow their energies and hostilities were channeled into constructive activities. Out of the group today there is a well-known poet and novelist, two or three PhDs who are now holding positions in large universities. All of the group acknowledge their indebtedness to her for her interest and encouragement."[5]

She also supervised the campus radio and chaired the fine arts series at Moorhead State (the school's name had changed from Moorhead State Teacher's College to Moorhead State College in 1957). It was this arts series that led to an incident with

1 "BPW to Hold 32nd Convention May 18-20," Bismarck *Tribune* (ND), May 10, 1951, 5.

2 "Air Passenger Manifest," *Selected Passenger and Crew Lists and Manifests.* National Archives, Washington, D.C. Northwest Airlines Inc., Aircraft No 74601, Flight No. 702, Sept 15, 1951.

3 "General Declaration, Customs, Immigration, and Public Health," The National Archives at Washington, D.C.; Washington, D.C.; *Passenger and Crew Lists of Vessels Arriving At Astoria, Portland, and Other Oregon Ports, Apr. 1888-Oct. 1956, and Passenger Lists of Airplanes Arriving At Portland, Oregon, Nov. 1948-Oct. 1952, Portland and Astoria*; NAI: 4497940; Record Group Title: *Records of the Immigration and Naturalization Service, 1787-2004*; Record Group Number: *85,* Northwest Airlines Inc., Aircraft No 74601, Flight No. 702, Sept, 1, 1951.

4 "Air Passenger Manifest," Flight No. 702, Sept 15, 1951.

5 "Delsie Holmquist speech about Catherine Cater, to NDSU Blue Key Fraternity Banquet, for Blue Key Doctor of Service Award, 1970," File 44, Catherine Cater Collection, North Dakota State University Institute for Regional Studies & Universities Archives, Fargo, ND, 3.

the Condells that festered for many years. The Condells were living in Fergus Falls and they had tickets to a concert at Moorhead State when Catherine was director of the fine arts series. The concert had been canceled but they had not been notified, so they made the trip. When they arrived, Catherine said on behalf of the school that she was sorry, but the college had to cancel the event. Yvonne Condell said, "I'm afraid I don't have the same favorable feelings about Catherine that others do. She was a little putting down to us. She said, 'I hope you'll come to something else we have on campus.' I found that down putting, so my introduction was not a pleasant one. She was a little snippy."[1] Still, people frequently confused the two academic powerhouse women. The day I spoke with Dr. Condell she said, "Just last week someone came up to me and said, 'Dr. Cater.' That's happened to me for the 50 years I've lived in Moorhead."[2]

Life for Catherine became more solitary in 1958. Now that she was single, her father had remained the constant figure she had turned to since her youth, though perhaps not in a completely open fashion. He had been a great influence on stimulating her interest in classical scholarship and literature. The NAACP publication, *The Crisis*, reported, "Dean James Tate Cater died of heart attack at his home in Whittier California on May 5, came to Talladega College as dean in fall of 1918, served in that capacity until June 2, 1952."[3]

Catherine's father's death was followed by his cremation at the Mountain View Cemetery and Mausoleum in Altadena, California.[4] He was 68, and left behind two documented children by his second wife, James T.J. and Sidney, along with Catherine by his first wife. This raises a question about Richard, whom Catherine referred to as her brother as did people who knew her, or knew about her, and spoke of her visiting him in the Southwest.[5]

1 Yvonne Condell, interview with Robert Dodge.
2 Ibid.
3 *The Crisis*, October 1958, 514.
4 State of California. *California Death Index, 1940-1997*. Sacramento, CA, USA: State of California Department of Health Services, Center for Health Statistics, *Find A Grave*. Find A Grave. http://www.findagrave.com/cgi-bin/fg.cgi.
5 Lou Richardson, interview with Robert Dodge, spoke of how Catherine liked to visit Richard, the "only one I ever heard her talk about." Yvonne Condell in interview said, "She has a brother who lives

Catherine had become well-established in the Fargo-Moorhead academic scene. In 1960 she was the speaker at the Phi Beta Kappa Banquet across the river in Fargo at North Dakota State University. Not surprisingly, her topic came from Greek mythology and the title of her talk was "Footnote to Daedalus." The NDSU *Spectrum* reported Catherine's talk as beginning by telling the story of Daedalus. Daedalus was a Greek architect who designed a labyrinth to hold the king's prisoners. This king was Minos of Crete, and the prisoners were the offspring of his queen and the Bull of Poseidon.[1] Daedalus angered the king and was confined to the labyrinth he had planned, along with his son, Icarus. The labyrinth was so well designed that Daedalus and Icarus could not find a way out. Eventually Daedalus used feathers and wax to attach wings to their bodies so they could fly upward to escape. Daedalus warned his son to not fly too near the sun or close to water, but to take a middle course. Icarus was exhilarated by flying, and kept going up and came so near sun that the wax melted, and his wings fell off, sending him to perish in the sea[2].

Catherine used this story to represent all humanity. She said people build labyrinths out of which they cannot escape. Humans have a "responsibility to be wise."[3] She contended that wisdom is more than knowledge, and more than retention of material. It is using knowledge for the betterment of all. As in the tragedy of Icarus, it is important to take the middle road, and be careful to not be so absorbed in what we are doing, to get a clear picture of the total experience.[4]

---

in Arizona, Richard. I heard she was down in Arizona visiting her brother."
1 David Leeming, *The Oxford Companion to World Mythology*, (New York: Oxford University Press, 2005), 91.
2 Ibid and "Dr. Cater Speaks at Phi Kappa Phi Banquet," *Spectrum* (NDSU), May 13, 1960, 4," File 33, Catherine Cater Collection, North Dakota State University Institute for Regional Studies & Universities Archives, Fargo, ND.
3 "Dr. Cater Speaks at Phi Kappa Phi Banquet".
4 Ibid.

CHAPTER 9. DISCORD, AND A MOVE ACROSS THE RIVER

Catherine remained at Moorhead State from the fall of 1949 through the spring of 1962. Hannah Vanorny's 2005 interview conveys a mixed message of the end of Catherine's Moorhead career. She says that Catherine's time there ended after 13 years with her "eventually walking out on Neumaier,"[1] referring to the president of the college at the time. Following that, Vanorny says Catherine left to cross the river to NDSU, since it was "bigger and seemed to offer more opportunities."[2] This makes it sound as though she decided to leave to seek a better position with greater prospects. I was in high school at the time, but I remember there being some controversy surrounding this. It appears that Catherine, for a second time, resigned her position at her college over a matter of principle.

Her colleagues recall Catherine's exodus from Moorhead State as having been a choice she made that involved some disagreement. "There was some sort of altercation. I think they put in some sort of requirement she just didn't want to fulfill, I just can't remember," recalled Lou Richardson.[3] Was it to seek

1 Vanorny, interview of Catherine Cater, Tape A.
2 Ibid.
3 Lou Richardson, Lou and Jerry Richardson, interview with Robert

greater opportunities? Lou replied, "No, no."[1] Jerry Richardson had a vague recollection it was about the president, Neumaier, and something that was a political, philosophical disagreement.[2] Steve Ward said, "There was some sort of arrangement with the college, with Moorhead State, and she thought they had let her down, and she was unhappy."[3] Mike Morrissey's account of Catherine's leaving is, "She was angry, disillusioned. There had been some incident that Morrissey could no longer specify, commenting, "There was, and I don't recall, whether it was a gender issue or a racial issue."[4]

Speaking about his beginning at Moorhead State, Neumaier commented, "I did feel very strongly . . . that when people learn English, or biology or a foreign language . . . that they should learn what has to be learned, and not at a second rate level. I'm afraid that was not only the case, but that was accepted, and I hoped that with the kind of faculty that we were going to attract and retain . . . that we were going to change that."[5] He obviously failed at retaining one member of the faculty who was raising standards.

Getting a new job at North Dakota State University came quickly. According to her 2005 interview, Catherine took a train to a humanities conference in Chicago following the incident. At a Minneapolis stop a man came over to her who may have been headed to the same conference. He was Seth Russell, the dean of NDSU's College of Humanities and Social Sciences,[6] who apparently was familiar with her outstanding capabilities. Dean Russell told her to go over to North Dakota State University to see John Hove and tell him to hire her. John Hove was head of the

---

Dodge, October, 9, 1015, Fargo, ND.
1 Ibid, Lou Richardson.
2 Ibid, Jerry Richardson.
3 Steve Ward, interview with Robert Dodge, October 11, 2015, Fargo, ND.
4 Ibid.
5 John Neumaier, "reflecting in a 1987 interview, on his ideas for further developing Moorhead State College after becoming the seventh president of the college in 1958," Moorhead State University Archives, Moorhead, MN, https://www.mnstate.edu/university-archives/125th-anniversary/1960s/.
6 Mike Nowatzki, "Tri-College to Celebrate 35th Anniversary: Founding Member George Sinner Retires From Board," *Forum* (Fargo), Jul 6, 2004.

English Department at North Dakota State University. Catherine took Russell's suggestion and Hove offered her a job, which she accepted.[1]

Morrissey's memory of this is, "She was leaving Moorhead on a train and ran into John Hove, who was either getting on, or there to meet somebody. They knew each other; he asked some questions about what she was doing. She said she had quit her job at Moorhead State and he literally hired her on the spot."[2] I personally have a recollection of John Hove's glee when he spoke of having Catherine land at NDSU after she had established such a stellar reputation as a teacher at Moorhead State and in the community as a scholar.

She was moving across the Red River to Fargo, North Dakota, the largest city in the state with a 1960 population of 47,000, and the center of the Fargo-Moorhead metropolitan area that numbered 106, 027.[3] The National Municipal League and *Look* Magazine had named Fargo an All American City in 1959, when building permits totaled $79,000,000.[4] NDSU was a different institution that attracted students from the very sparsely populated state, where educational preparation for college varied. She was moving to a state land grant university, where it appeared standards might be a step down from her years at Olivet and the niche she had created at Moorhead State. The 1960 North Dakota's average income was $1,741, only 78% the national average.[5] Though one-room schools had declined considerably, there were still 1,143,[6] while many rural teachers had one year or less of college training. Only 16 of 53 county superintendents of school had completed a four-year college course.[7] High school accreditation standards were not a high bar to meet, requiring three teachers instructing students in their majors and minors and a minimum of 25 students for minor accreditation, and four

---

1 Vanorny, interview of Catherine Cater, Tape A.
2 Mike Morrissey interview October 9, 2015.
3 "Demographics," *City of Fargo*, http://www.cityoffargo.com/CityInfo/Demographics.aspx.
4 Elwyn B. Robinson, *History of North Dakota* (Lincoln: University of Nebraska Press, 1966), 453.
5 Ibid.
6 Ibid, 483.
7 Ibid., 485.

teachers instructing students in their majors and minors for full accreditation. In 1960 the state had 352 high schools, and 199 received minor accreditation while only 137 were fully accredited.[1]

By a constitutional amendment approved by voters on December 8, 1960, North Dakota Agricultural College's name was changed to North Dakota State University of Agriculture and Applied Sciences.[2] The school's mascot was the Bison. My recollection is that when I enrolled in 1963 tuition was $500 per quarter and the university was on a three quarter regular school year. The reasonable price of the public institution and the standards of North Dakota high school education when Catherine moved to North Dakota State made the level of students she would encounter in freshman English less prepared than those she had dealt with at Olivet, and perhaps marginally less prepared than at Moorhead State; though when John Neumaier became president of Moorhead State in 1958 he felt the students were receiving a second rate education, compared to students in the Twin Cities of Minneapolis-St. Paul.[3]

Catherine made the move to North Dakota, where the state coat of arms is an Indian arrowhead that symbolizes the "Sioux State"[4] and the banner underneath declares "Strength from the Soil."[5] She had spent her early years in the South surrounded by cotton "plantations," and in 1962 she found her permanent academic home, which would be the pancake flat Red River valley, once the bottom of glacial Lake Agassiz surrounded by rich farmland that grew wheat in abundance as well other crops. She was heading to what had been begun as an agricultural college, which remained a primary focus, with engineering as its second strength. It hardly seemed a perfect fit for an English Literature PhD with a thorough background in philosophy

1 Ibid., 485.
2 Robinson, *History of North Dakota*, 499.
3 John Neumaier, "reflecting in a 1987 interview, on his ideas for further developing Moorhead State College," Moorhead State University Archives.
4 "State Coat of Arms," North Dakota.gov, http://www.nd.gov/content.htm?parentCatID=74&id=State%20Coat%20of%20Arms.
5 Ibid.

CHAPTER 10. NORTH DAKOTA STATE, THE EARLY YEARS

Catherine began her career at North Dakota State University in the fall of 1962. The football season's embarrassing start would be overshadowed by world events. For the nation and for the world it was a perilous time. The Cold War that had created a Sword of Damocles hanging over humanity since the development of thermonuclear weapons and intercontinental missiles reached a climax. On the evening of October 22, President Kennedy went on television and declared, "Within the past week, unmistakable evidence has established the fact that a series of offensive missile sites is now in preparation [in Cuba]. The purpose of these bases can be none other than to provide a nuclear strike capability against the Western Hemisphere."[1] He announced a blockade of Cuba and said, "Any nuclear missile launched from Cuba against any nation in the Western Hemisphere will be regarded as an attack by the Soviet Union on the United States, requiring a full retaliatory response upon the Soviet Union."[2] The thirteen day Cuban missile crisis that begin-

---

1 "Radio and Television Report to the American People on the Soviet Arms Buildup in Cuba, October 22, 1962," John F Kennedy Presidential Library and Museum. http://www.jfklibrary.org/Asset-Viewer/sU-VmCh-sB0moLfrBcaHaSg.aspx.
2 Ibid.

ning in late October 1962, was, according to historian Arthur Schlesinger, "not only the most dangerous moment of the Cold War, it was the most dangerous moment in human history."[1]

Longtime historian at the John F. Kennedy Library, Sheldon Stern, reported the nation's reaction to Kennedy's speech: "The American public responded to JFK's speech with some signs of panic. Food and emergency supplies disappeared from supermarkets and hardware stores. Long lines were reported at gasoline stations, and there was a run on tires. People across America stood in silent, worried clumps around newsstands, anxiously reading the latest headlines. At the Phillips Academy in Andover, Mass., and at the Mount Hermon School to the west, students received phone calls from their parents urging them to come home to be with their families—just in case. Some 10 million Americans also left the nation's cities hoping to find safety 'far away from nuclear targets.' "[2]

During that fall, so memorable for the Cuban Missile Crisis, Mike Morrissey's time coincided with the start of Catherine's career at NDSU. After graduating with his "practical" English degree at NDSU in December of 1962 and unable to find a teaching job, Mike had returned to his family's home in St. Paul to work in a plant, bottling 7-Up. John Hove, the head of the English Department, contacted him and asked if he would be interested in returning to NDSU to pursue graduate work, suggesting he could finance it by teaching freshman English. Mike returned to Fargo in the fall of '63, and it was then that he met Catherine. He recollected that the first course he had from her was "Writers of the Regional South," and adds, "She was the most amazing teacher I had ever experienced."[3]

It was an intimidating experience for Mike as he started, having only graduated the previous year. He was in an office full of people who had just been his professors and were currently

1 Arthur M. Schlesinger Jr., *A Thousand Days: John F. Kennedy in the White House* (New York: Mariner Books, 2002), xiv.
2 Sheldon M. Stern, The Week the World Stood Still: Inside the Secret Cuban Missile Crisis (Palo Alto, CA: Stanford University Press, 2004), 91–92.
3 Mike Morrissey, interview with Robert Dodge, Fargo, ND, Oct 9, 2015.

his mentors in graduate classes. "I felt way out of my league,"[1] he said, and also fascinated, limited by his background. Mike soon found he had desk in the large space where Catherine and other teachers hung out when not in classes. "It was a desk I hesitated to occupy as I was so recent a graduate from all these different instructors."[2]

The English Department that Catherine joined was academically strong. There was Shakespeare authority Francis Schoff, Leonard Sackett, Ralph Engel, whose service would be recognized by a scholarship for an English major established in his name,[3] along with a number of teachers aides. Department chairman John Hove was a linguist who taught American Literature and was an American Studies PhD from the University of Minnesota. He was soon to be the unsuccessful Democratic nominee for the House of Representatives from Eastern North Dakota in the 1964 election.

The very formidable Rhode's Scholar, Thomas McGrath, came to NDSU the same year as Catherine. It was the year his best-known work, *Letters to an Imaginary Friend*, was first released. McGrath was a nationally known poet who, after serving in the army in World War II, spent time at Los Angeles State University, where he wrote film and television scripts. He had been dismissed from the university following an appearance as an unfriendly witness before the House Un-American Activities Committee in 1953.[4] Catherine had left Olivet in protest over Red Scare intrusion on their campus, but Tom McGrath had been openly defiant and would be "tainted" from then on, though both NDSU and Moorhead State would hire him. McGrath began his statement to HUAC with the comment, "After a dead serious consideration of the effects of this committee's work and of my relation to it, I find that for the following reasons I must refuse to cooperate with this body," then cited

1 Ibid.
2 Mike Morrissey, interview.
3 "Professor Ralph Engle Scholarship" – awarded to a major who has completed at least 21 credits at NDSU, https://www.ndsu.edu/english/ourprogram/.
4 "Fredrick C. Stern, "A Biographical Sketch of Thomas McGrath," *Modern American Poetry*, http://www.english.illinois.edu/maps/poets/m_r/mcgrath/life.htm.

his responsibilities to his students, to his profession, as a poet, and his first amendment rights.[1] Following that, McGrath was blacklisted like many in the McCarthy era.[2] I recall, from having him as a teacher, that the book jacket of his poetry collection stated, "he was included on all of the better blacklists." The blacklisting damaged his career and his writing was never as recognized as it was critically acclaimed. Dr. Roland Dille, President of Minnesota State University, where McGrath taught after leaving NDSU in 1969, said, "He was a communist at one time. He was very left-wing, but so were many people from rural farming areas."[3] McGrath eventually published over 20 books,[4] received two National Endowment for the Arts Fellowships and a Guggenheim Fellowship, was awarded an honorary Doctorate from the University of North Dakota and won an award from the Associated Writing Programs that included a tribute presented by "Studs" Terkel.[5]

But coming into this strong department, Catherine was still Catherine. There were a number of women teaching English with assistantships like Mike, and he did not think any prejudice against women existed on the English faculty. Jerry Richardson noted that some in Agriculture and Engineering viewed the group as extremely left wing, and if the English Department had any questions about Catherine's racial background, they were the least likely group to have been bothered.[6] Mike said that when Catherine first began working at NDSU, everything seemed very professional, but later her relationship with John Hove became strained. The problem was "Catherine thought maybe he had hired someone into the department that had taken some of his spotlight." He thought there might have been some jealousy, which was very surprising to Mike, who considered Hove to be a mentor also. Mike added, "For Catherine to share

1 "McGrath's Statement to the House Committee on Un-American Activities," Modern American Poetry, http://www.english.illinois.edu/maps/poets/m_r/mcgrath/huac.htm
2 "Thomas McGrath; Poet Was Blacklisted in '50s," Los Angeles *Times*, September 24, 1990.
3 Jeremy Perleberg, "Thomas McGrath: Politics and Poetry," *Horisonslines. org*, http://www.horizonlines.org/Volume1/inprint/mcgrath.html.
4 Ibid.
5 Stern, "A Biographical Sketch of Thomas McGrath".
6 Jerry Richardson, interview Oct 19, 2015.

with me this other side of John was very conflicting to me."[1]

Being in Catherine's courses, Mike said, "The first thing I realized was that a student could not give a wrong answer to Catherine. She had a way of turning a sow's ear into a silk purse."[2] He added, Catherine was, "more than supportive," which was why he asked her to be his advisor for his master's thesis. It was a good choice as she was, "Always helpful, always available, always willing to sit down and answer your questions to the very last one."[3]

Catherine described what NDSU was to her: "NDSU is a public institution to which students 17, 18 and on up as old as they get can actually talk with a professor without fear of condescension for the most part and where they can question not only their own thinking but question the ideas of other people."[4]

I soon discovered the truth of that statement. Her second year at NDSU was the year I met Catherine and was her student. She had been named a full professor by that time.[5] Because of Catherine Cater and being in her classes, I went on to other institutions of higher education and had many outstanding professors. But never was there anyone who was her equal in managing a class and raising its level, inspiring the confidence of those involved, instilling such a desire to become a scholar. I briefly became an English major so I could have her as my advisor and spend more time around her, talking, learning, just being in her company.

Her former student and colleague Steve Ward described Catherine's teaching style:

> She had two modes. One was a kind of asking. She would ask questions and she would celebrate the answers, no matter what the answers would be. She said, "Yes!" She'd call on somebody, she'd say, "Did you read the material?" Yes. "And what did you think of it?" I

1 Mike Morrissey, interview.
2 Ibid.
3 Ibid.
4 Excerpts: Catherine Cater," NDSU Magazine, Fall 2000, Vol. 01, No.1, Box 1, Folder 37, Catherine Cater Collection, North Dakota State University Archives, Fargo, ND.
5 Vanorny, interview of Catherine Cater, Tape A.

thought it was interesting. "Yes! And what did you think was interesting?" The next thing you know she's got you going so deep into the material, you're saying things that you didn't know you knew. She was just great that way.

That was one thing. The other thing was that she was always allusive. So when she was done finding out what you thought, she would connect it to other things, and she would say, "You will remember," then she would mention some obscure book that no one had ever heard of. Oh yes, oh yes, we would remember that, then we would write it down and maybe when we got out of class, we'd read it at some time.

So she had this thing. Not only did she have 10,000 books, she had us lugging books everywhere, out of the library and out of the bookstores. So, those two things, asking questions and being allusive. She was so good at that.[1]

Lou and Jerry Richardson also arrived in Fargo in 1963, and they were among those who would become lifelong close friends with Catherine from that point on. Both were from South Dakota, and they met at South Dakota State University, where they married the day after graduation. Following a stint in Korea at the end of the Korean War, Jerry was hired as an assistant in publications and sports information at South Dakota State. By the time Jerry was offered the communications job at NDSU, they had four children, and Lou was sick of being a housewife. She began a master's degree program in English, and had her first course from Catherine, which was Southern Literature.[2] She followed that by taking courses on Chaucer, Milton and "if she taught more, I would have taken it."[3] One thing she recalls that surprised her from the intellectual Catherine is that when Lou was enrolled in her classes, occasionally Catherine would make allusions to having watched the soap operas over the noon

1 Steve Ward interview.
2 Lou Richardson, interview, Oct 19, 2015.
3 Ibid.

hours.[1] It was a side of her one would not expect, but it showed up again later, and not all had to be cerebrally profound for her.

Lou was a teacher's aide her second year and taught Freshman English. She hoped to join the English faculty after completing her master's degree, but the Journalism teacher had resigned by that time and the Dean, Seth Russell, needed a replacement. Journalism had been Lou's major at South Dakota State University and with her English master's degree she appeared qualified. She was offered the position and began her 27 years on the faculty. She then became a colleague of both Catherine and Jerry.[2]

In 1964, Delsie Holmquist followed Catherine from Moorhead State to NDSU. Catherine had lived in a two-story brick building on 10th Street North during her first years in Fargo. When Delsie came, they got a small rambler home at 1425 10th Street North[3] that would remain a permanent part of Catherine's life from then on. This is when she began her closer, mutually dependent relationship with Delsie. In addition to teaching English courses, Catherine developed what Paul Homan described as "a course which would become legendary at NDSU. 'Approach to the Humanities' was a year-long interdisciplinary survey of the arts and humanities which attracted students from every corner of the campus, and for which she and Delsie literally traveled the world collecting course materials." Travel became a major source of enjoyment and continuing education for Catherine.

In Catherine's early years as an instructor at NDSU, one of those who had her as a teacher was Ene Kõivastik Vogel. Ene was not an English major but had heard of Catherine and chose to try electives that she offered. Ene recalls, "Walking into her class, Catherine was full of life, enthusiasm for her subject, enthusiasm for her students wanting to learn, eager to listen to students. She asked many questions, she allowed discussion, there were never any putdowns in class. I remember people feeling a little intimidated at the beginning of class, particularly if it was the first one you took from her. She quickly took care of that. You felt that Catherine knew you as a young person, and

---

1 Ibid.
2 Lou and Jerry Richardson, interview, Oct 19, 2015
3 *1993-2002 White Pages*, Acxiom Corporation, Little Rock, AR, *Fargo*; State: *North Dakota*; Year(s): 1993, 1994, 1995.

not just a student she was required to have in class."[1]

Another of Catherine's students in her very first NDSU years was Pat Dodge Stocker. Pat was an English major who was a junior when Catherine arrived, and she took three courses from the new English professor. One she mentioned was offered for graduate credit, and involved writing a major paper. She recalls, "I laugh a bit now when I remember the written comment she made on my paper—'a good start on a very difficult subject.' I thought it was a compliment, and only later, on reflection, did I realize that it really wasn't. However, it seemed to work well as feedback, and I 'borrowed' that phrase many times later in life when I was a professor myself."[2] That reflects something true of Catherine, that she had demanding standards. These were the days before grade inflation, but Catherine always valued academic rigor, and somehow managed to make students believe they were capable of achieving it.

Her grading and interest in students is captured in a story my mother told me years ago. She became a friend of Catherine's through the American Association of University Women and other local activities. Back in the 1950s and 60s my mother had been the secretary at Agassiz Junior High School on the south side of Fargo, where she also taught mathematics at times for students who found the subject especially challenging. In one of her math classes she had a personable student who went on to finish high school at Fargo Central, then graduate from NDSU and become a successful Fargo businessman. I was visiting Fargo and talking to my mom about Catherine, when she told me about running into her former student at the bank, where they caught up on old times. He mentioned his years at NDSU and brought up Catherine as his favorite teacher, describing his course from her as "the best D I ever had."

Along with making lasting impressions on students from her first year at North Dakota State, Catherine began broadening the school's cultural horizon. In her very early years she was instrumental in instituting a new policy of assigning a book as summer reading for all incoming freshman. At orientation there

1 Ene Kõivastik Vogel, telephone interview with Robert Dodge, Nov. 18, 2015.
2 Pat Stocker email to Robert Dodge, Nov 18, 2015.

would be a lecture on the book by its author, followed by discussions in small groups led by faculty from all departments. The book gave all people on campus a common point of reference for sharing thoughts during their four undergraduate years.[1] She also was involved in initiating a speaker series that brought in noted intellectuals to share their ideas with the students and faculty. The choice of those invited was obviously Catherine's.

The first speaker was Ashley Montagu,[2] who was in the vanguard of early scholars to challenge eugenics thinking. His 1942 book, *Man's Most Dangerous Myth: The Fallacy of Race*,[3] was groundbreaking in America for denying the concept of race. The opening sentence of his book declared, "The idea of 'race' represents one of the most dangerous myths of our time, and one of the most tragic," and the paragraph closed with, "Race is the witchcraft, the demonology of our time, the means by which we exorcise imagined demonical powers among us. It is the contemporary myth, humankind's most dangerous myth, America's Original Sin."[4]

Montagu's ideas obviously resonated with Catherine, who had known what it was to be regarded as inferior by others' racial classification, and she brought that message to Fargo at her first opportunity.

The next year's speaker was one of Catherine's greatest inspirations, Robert Hutchins. By this time Hutchins was no longer president of the University of Chicago, where his Great Books curriculum and Socratic methodology had influenced Catherine's father and been adapted to her undergraduate education. At Chicago he had dropped the school out of the Big Ten football conference, and in 1939 convinced the school to drop football, as he said, "In many colleges, it is possible for a boy to win 12 letters without learning how to write one."[5] Football was just beginning to take on great importance at NDSU but Catherine did not share the growing enthusiasm. When Hutchins

---

1 Vanorny, interview of Catherine Cater, Tape A.
2 Lou and Jerry Richardson, interview.
3 Ashley Montagu, *Man's Most Dangerous Myth: The Fallacy of Race* (New York: Harpers, 1942).
4 Ibid., 1.
5 Barry Bearak, "Where Football and Higher Education Mix," New York *Times*, Sept 17, 2011, D1.

appeared at NDSU, he was head of the Center for the Study of Democratic Institutions, chairman of the Board of Editors of *Encyclopedia Britannica*, coeditor with Mortimer Adler of an annual, *The Great Ideas Today*, and had been editor-in-chief of the 54-volume *Great Books of the Western World*.[1] He was an influential intellectual and this was Catherine's one opportunity in her life to meet Hutchins, the man she admired so much.[2]

It was a series that did not continue, but Catherine would be given other opportunities for bringing in speakers in the future.

Her overall academic scholarship made her a logical choice to be in charge of the team when NDSU was selected in 1966 to be a contestant on the popular Sunday afternoon TV quiz show, *GE College Bowl*. *College Bowl* was an Emmy winning quiz show first on CBS, but then on NBC by 1964. It matched teams of four people from two different colleges in a contest to answer a wide range of academic questions. The format was that the host, who was Robert Earle at the time NDSU was to participate,[3] would ask what was called a tossup question, which was answered by whoever pushed a buzzer the fastest. That could get points for his team. If that answer was incorrect the other team had a chance to try to answer. Answering the tossup question correctly allowed the chance to answer a bonus question for that team to gain more points.

Tryouts were held in the spring of 1966 in the Student Union before a panel of professors from various colleges. Individuals were called into a room one at a time and asked questions. There was a large turnout of applicants, as the show was popular and those selected would receive a trip to New York City. Following the tryouts eight people were chosen. The person who had the best results in English, science, history, and one with a more general background, had been named as the final team, and the four next highest were chosen for practice matches to be conducted throughout the summer. I was one of the second four, which meant I would be seeing Catherine once a week all sum-

1 "John Maynard Hutchins: American Educator," *Encyclopedia Britannica*, http://www.britannica.com/biography/Robert-Maynard-Hutchins.
2 Jerry Richardson, interview.
3 other College Bowl hosts included Art Fleming, Pat Sajak, Allen Ludden, Dick Cavett.

mer. We were all given copies of the *Columbia Desk Encyclopedia*, the Google of its day, plus various materials. The Engineering department built us electronic boards with buzzers for our practice sessions. When fall came Catherine announced that the team was to include one alternate in case anyone became ill. She added that I had been the strongest performer in our practice sessions, so would be going to New York as a member of the College Bowl team.

We flew to New York several days early and Catherine enjoyed showing us around, walking us through Greenwich Village, taking us to a performance of *The Fantasticks*, and strolling though Central Park. It was great fun being with Catherine in New York, where she was very comfortable in the urban area with all the culture, and knew how to cope and deal with people. The College Bowl contest was on NBC on October 2, 1966, against repeat winner, the University of Oklahoma. Everyone was well, so I watched from the audience as NDSU was trounced by a score of 375-45.[1]

It was not the result anyone had hoped for; perhaps since the football team had won successive North Central Conference championships in 1964, 65 and 66[2] people thought academics would follow. Catherine later said that when she coached the NDSU College Bowl team, they froze against Oklahoma and maybe she could have tried to get them to be more aggressive in pushing the buzzers.[3] Perhaps she could have, but at most that might have altered the margin of defeat by a small amount. By being more aggressive the team might have never escaped the negative score it had at the halfway point in the game, since there were penalties for incorrect answers. It was a simple case of competing against a superior team that had experience. She added that upon our return, NDSU President Albrecht was upset with the result.[4]

---

1 "GE College Bowl TV Show History," http://www.collegebowl.com/ schoolhistoryrpt.asp?CustomerID=252.
2 "NDSU Historical Facts," North Dakota State Archives.
3 Vanorny, interview of Catherine Cater, Tape A.
4 Ibid.

CHAPTER 11. SCHOLARS, ENLIGHTENMENT

Catherine on the North Dakota State University campus (North Dakota State University Photo)

The 1960s were marked by great social upheaval and activism, as the Vietnam War escalated abroad and the civil rights movement gained traction in the U.S., with the moderate faction led by Martin Luther King being challenged by militants demanding more rapid change. All who knew Catherine saw her as a liberal, but she was rarely described as an activist in the great forces that were shaping the times. It was part of that mystery she had adopted and maintained about herself, that while she was not in causes like some of her colleagues in academia in the later 1960s, she certainly was aware of issues and approached them from her philosophical background.

NDSU was not at the forefront of activism, but during my senior year Ralph Abernathy of the Southern Christian Leadership Conference visited the campus to speak. There was a reception following at the Student Union where I was among many who went to meet him. Martin Luther King, Jr. described Abernathy as his "best friend,"[1] and the two worked extremely closely in the civil rights movement. If Catherine attended, I do not recall her being there, and her presence is something I rarely failed to notice. She certainly was not prominent in any way at the event. Several years later, immediately following the Kent State shootings, Dick Gregory spoke to a packed house at Festival Hall. I brought a small group of students from West Fargo, where I had begun my teaching career, and again have no recollection of Catherine being in the audience, though I sought to greet her.

This is in keeping with the view of Catherine as observed by her former student and colleague, Stephen Disrud. He said, "I never saw her as a political animal, but of course she cared about those humanistic values, such as social justice, as it applied to individuals, as it applied as ideas. But in a lot of ways I see her as an anti-political animal. I saw her as an intellectual and beyond that. She was interested in the ideas, a student of the mind."[2]

To Yvonne Condell, it is more likely a part of the continuing denial she saw in Catherine as an abandonment of her heritage. Yvonne was well aware of whom Catherine had married, and his accomplishments in breaking barriers for African-Americans. She also spoke of an African-American veterinarian and his wife who had moved to Fargo. Yvonne stated, "His wife was a class-

---

1 Adelle M. Banks, "Rev. Ralph Abernathy: Martin Luther King, Jr.'s Overlooked 'Civil Rights Twin," *Huffington Post*, Nov 20, 2015, http://www.huffingtonpost.com/2015/01/19/rev-ralph-abernathy-civil-rights_n_6482176.html.
2 Stephen Disrud interview with Robert Dodge, Fargo, ND, October 13, 2015.

mate or a schoolmate of Catherine's in Talladega in Alabama. She tried several times to get in touch with Catherine and Catherine did not respond."[1] It was part of the mystery Catherine chose to maintain until she reached 98.

Catherine's view of the humanities governed her life in many ways. As she explained to Hannah Vanorny, what was commonly thought was that a greater understanding of the humanities could/should teach people what the human condition is, and to know ways in which they could improve the world. Both of these ideas, she said, are erroneous. For evidence, she noted that Hitler's advisors were educated. Humanities, in Catherine's words, "help people live with themselves in their own way. I don't know what else there is."[2]

Catherine's love of humanities was to lead her to a crowning achievement in 1968. That tumultuous year the Democratic National Convention went through periods of anarchy, as crowds chanted, "The Whole World's Watching," and there were displays of Black militancy by U.S. athletes at the Olympics. The musical *Hair* captured the generation gap by celebrating long hair, drugs, and nudity. Two inspirational Americans, Martin Luther King Jr. and Robert Kennedy, were assassinated, and public opinion turned more and more against the Vietnam War. The autumn brought Richard Nixon to power as president in a close election.

Amid this turmoil, Catherine attended her first meeting of the National Collegiate Honors Association.[3] This organization's mission is, "To support and enhance the community of educational institutions, professionals, and students who participate in collegiate honors education around the world."[4] Catherine had decided to add an honors program to the NDSU campus, and she became very active with the National Collegiate Honors Council, regularly attending the annual meetings to share information and set agendas for policy, serving on nearly all the major committees and chairing the publications board. In 1974 she was

---

1 Yvonne Condell interview.
2 Vanorny, interview of Catherine Cater, Tape A.
3 Paul Homan, "A Humanist in Honors," 89.
4 "Mission," National Collegiate Honors Association, http://nchchonors.org.

elected national president of the organization.[1]

Catherine introduced an honors program at NDSU in the fall of 1968,[2] but chose to call it the Scholars Program. She had selected the name "Scholars," rather than the more common "Honors," because she thought Honors would be seen as elitist.[3] Regardless of the name, the program led to a disagreement between her and her department chairman, John Hove, who thought the program was elitist. Catherine's response to him was that of course it was, as it properly should be. So too was the football team and the choir. It was appropriate to should show respect for intellectual activities, and do so by bringing together those who posses it, offer an interdisciplinary approach, then they could have discussions appropriate for a university.[4] What may have been Catherine's most enduring single legacy to North Dakota State University was born.

Dean Thomas Riley arrived after the program was well established, but the issue of elitism had not passed. He wrote:

> I hoped for an enhancement of the honors program, but there was considerable opposition to this as an elitist move. Many faculty thought that an honors program that welcomed anyone who felt they could master the courses offered should be welcomed into it. I still believe that an honors program that cultivates the best and most dedicated students is the best model, and that it should also do its best to get those students Rhodes Scholarships, Truman, Goldwater and other fellowships to graduate school, as well as groom them for the opportunities such as international study and the highest ranked law, medical and graduate schools. But faculty have to buy into such a model. I still don't know where Catherine stood on this issue, but I know that she never actively cultivated strife on the campus. She believed that we could always talk our way to reasonable compromise.[5]

---

1 Paul Homan, "A Humanist in Honors," 89.
2 "Biography," Finding Aid to Catherine Cater Papers, NDSU Institute for Regional Studies & Universities Archives, Fargo, ND, 3.
3 Paul Homan interview with Robert Dodge, Fargo, ND, Oct 13, 2015.
4 Vanorny, interview of Catherine Cater, Tape A.
5 Thomas Riley Email to Robert Dodge, October 15, 2015,

Initially this was Catherine's program, beginning with about 30 students housed in a "homey" location in Southeast Engineering.[1] From the beginning it was all inter-disciplinary seminars that drew faculty from across the various faculties on campus. This made it compatible with any major. It provided an intimate forum in which students could learn with Catherine, and she gained a generation of grateful admirers. Steve Ward was a teacher in the early years of the program. He said that Catherine's idea for the program was, "Put good students in a room together with good teachers and have them read good books and talk about them. And that's what we did."[2] Deborah Kaseman described the experience with Catherine in the early years of the program in a way that all who have known her would have always described her: "She has a way of coming across to people that is not condescending, even though you feel she knows so much more than you do."[3]

The appearance of a wealthy donor would provide the Scholars Program a new home, and soon offer Catherine another opportunity to bring added culture to the community. He was Rueben Askanase, an immigrant's son who was born in Fargo in 1908 to Fisel and Rose (Graham) Askanase. Fisel was an itinerate peddler with a shop at 86 Front Street,[4] and young Rueben helped take care of his family by assisting his mother in providing meals for railroad workers,[5] or in their chuck wagon, as they followed migrant workers, cooking and serving them meals when they toiled, and sometimes boarding them.[6] After working his way through what was then North Dakota Agricultural College (NDSU), he went from office boy to vice president of the New York department store, Abraham and Strauss. He then moved to Houston in 1945, where he and his partners built a company into Dunhill International, which owned Spaulding sporting goods and other properties. By the early 1960s, Askanase was chairman

---

1 Paul Homan interview.
2 Steve Ward interview with Robert Dodge, Fargo, ND, Oct 11, 2015.
3 Kosse, "Cater: 'infect one another with the desire to learn,' ".
4 Curk Ericksmoen, "Fargo Native a Big Success in Business," *Bismarck Tribune*, Apr 4, 2010.
5 Ibid.
6 "Askanase, Reuben W.," *Texas State Historical Association*, https://tsha-online.org/handbook/online/articles/fasph.

of the board of New York Dock Railway, Coty Cosmetics, and more.[1]

A campaign began in the 1960s to raise $350,000 to build a new Little Country Theater at North Dakota State in a building that would also house the Speech and Drama Department.[2] The Development Foundation files of the NDSU Archives list Rueben Askanase and his wife making a $100,000 contribution to the university.[3] This likely explains the naming of the building, the Askanase Hall, which opened in 1968.[4] He also created Askanase scholarships at NDSU.[5]

Askanase Hall became the home of the Scholars Program as the number enrolled in it expanded, and soon the program was given a department designation for some of its courses.[6]

While the Askanase Hall was in the process of being built, Jerry Richardson had come to know Askanase through his job in publications at NDSU. Jerry had visited Askanase and his wife, Hilda, in Texas, and was sure that they would like Catherine, so he introduced them. He was correct, and Catherine visited the Askanase home in Houston. They became very fond of her, and after the Askanase Hall was complete they remained fans of Catherine. Her office was moved into the new building when it housed the Scholars Program.

Catherine never learned to drive, and through her NDSU years she walked to work from her 10th Street residence, which with North Dakota winters could be a real challenge. At one point Reuben contacted Jerry and asked, "Does she need a winter coat and a pair of shoes?"[7] When she heard about this, she

1 Ericksmoen, "Fargo Native a Big Success".
2 "Askanase Hall: Description," *Campus Office Directory*, North Dakota State University, https://www.ndsu.edu/alphaindex/buildings/Building::340.
3 Print Material Series, 7/7, 7/8, Finding Aid to the NDSU Development Foundation Records, NDSU Institute for Regional Studies & Universities Archives, Fargo, ND, http://library.ndsu.edu/repository/bitstream/handle/10365/395/DevelopmentFoundation-Records.pdf.
4 "NDSU Historical Facts," North Dakota State University Archives, http://library.ndsu.edu/ndsuarchives/ndsu-historical-facts.
5 "Askanase, Reuben W.," *Texas State Historical Association*.
6 Paul Homan interview.
7 Jerry Richardson interview, telephone interview with Jerry Richardson by Robert Dodge, November 17, 2015.

"snorted" with indignation. She felt capable of taking care of herself.[1] That would change.

Bill Cosgrove first met Catherine in December 1969 in what he describes as "a charming little alcove in one of the mezzanines of the Brown Palace Hotel in Denver during the MLA (Modern Language Association) Convention."[2] The purpose of this introduction was for him to interview for a job opening in American Literature at NDSU that Cosgrove believes had been Catherine's close friend, Delsie Holmquist's position, before she retired. He noted, "I was impressed by her calm yet engaging demeanor and sincere, personable way of relating to me. At the time, I preferred the open position at Moorhead State and the interview with 'Soc' Glasrud, but they didn't have the funds in the end."[3] Cosgrove was hired and became a longtime member of the NDSU English Department. During his first year, "We recall Catherine having a nice reception for us and another new assistant professor and spouse in 1970 at her duplex on north 10th Street in Fargo she shared with Delsie. And she had me in to talk to a class of hers about Faulkner and then, or later, gave me a couple valuable books on and about Faulkner which I used a lot and shared with my students, especially grad students."[4]

Catherine was always a Faulkner fan, and along with her PhD thesis, she spoke of her Southern background and referred to the writer in 1977 in an article published in the *Spectrum*. She was quoted as saying, "In a sense, the glimpse of extreme poverty and deprivation have helped to make me aware of some people's needs and the kind of survival that Faulkner and other Southern writers reflected."[5] In that article, the author reported, "Cater compares herself to Faulkner's character Quentin in that they were both 'hating it while trying to understand it'."[6] Quentin seems a dubious choice for Catherine to identify with. He is a character in Faulkner's *The Sound and the Fury*[7] whose once proud

---

1 Ibid.
2 Bill Cosgrove Email to Robert Dodge, Oct 17, 2015.
3 Ibid.
4 Bill Cosgrove second Email to Robert Dodge, Oct 17, 2015.
5 Kosse, "Cater: 'infect one another with the desire to learn,' ".
6 Ibid.
7 William Faulkner, *The Sound and the Fury* (New York: Jonathan Cape and Harrison Smith, 1929).

family has fallen, and he rejects his father's values, though the world does not. In final frustration, he turns to suicide. Academic comment suggests that "[h]aunted by a past to which he is inadequate, dogged by a present he cannot face, and doomed to no future, Quentin, through his diction and general point of view—both what he speaks and what he thinks—dramatizes a modern yet universal sensibility."[1]

The year 1969 was notable in NDSU history. The school received national attention. While the football team was the national champion in Division II,[2] a more novel event captured coast-to-coast headlines during spring break. Reports of the origin of what happened differ, with Rob Kirkpatrick's *1969: The Year Everything Changed* crediting NDSU student body president Chuck Stroup with originating the idea,[3] a claim that was repeated recently in a *Spectrum* article of March 2015 by Jack Dura.[4] Stroup took out an ad in the paper supporting it, but a more accurate recounting of the origin of the idea and how it developed comes from former *Spectrum* editor Kevin Carvelle:

> When I was editor of the NDSU Spectrum in 1968–69, we had a tight knit staff. A lot of what we published was controversial (editorials and articles from a liberal perspective, several pieces on the growth of the drug culture, on the rise of feminism, etc.) and some we did not publish (articles on Greek social life) irritated certain segments of campus. As a result, we felt a mite beleaguered. This gave rise to the notion that we should celebrate the end of a stressful year with a staff picnic and overnight, and because of its unlikely name, Zap was settled on as the locale.

1 May Cameron Brown, "The Language of Chaos: Quentin Compson in the Sound and the Fury," *American Literature*, Vol. 51, No. 4, Jan 1980, 533.
2 "NDSU Historical Facts," Archives.
3 See Rob Kirkpatrick, *1969: The Year Everything Changed* (New York: Skyhorse Publishing, 2011), 87: "Chuck Stroup, North Dakota State University student body president in 1969, remembers that he went downstairs from his student government office to the offices of the NDSU student newspaper, the *Spectrum*, early that semester and suggested an idea for students who couldn't afford to make it to the traditional spring break destination of Florida."
4 Jack Dura, " 'A Helluva Good Time in Zap, North Dakota': From 1969's Zip to Zap to 2015, Spring Break Safety as Important as Ever," *Spectrum*, http://ndsuspectrum.com/a-helluva-good-time-in-zap-north-dakota/ March 12, 2015.

I began joking about it in the fine print in the masthead in March. At an early spring staff meeting someone mentioned that the Theta Chi fraternity (composed largely of men from Western North Dakota) wanted to come to Zap. Someone noted that the Vets Club (of which I had been a member) was also thinking of coming to Zap. Another person said the football team was interested. As a result, I concluded that our private joke of a Zip-to-Zap had become a public phenomenon. That meant it deserved news coverage and I and two old friends from Mott . . . drove to Zap and did a little reconnaissance to determine if Zap would be suitable. Upon our return, I wrote a goofy, tongue-in-cheek story about the upcoming event. [Kevin's full-page story ended with "a full program of orgies, brawls, freak outs, and arrests is being planned. Don't you dare miss it"[1]] But having avoided classes most of that spring semester, I was forced to drop out of school that same week and returned to Mott.

First, however, I printed a supply of Zip-to-Zap posters and traveled with a buddy, Russ Wahlum of Bismarck, to the State School of Science at Wahpeton, Mayville State, UND, Devils Lake Junior College, Minot State, and Valley City State too . . . At those schools I posted the fliers and met with the staffers of the school papers, encouraging them to provide publicity. I also was in contact with the newspaper staff at Dickinson State.

Meanwhile, the Associated Press decided that my story in *The Spectrum* was comic enough that it did a piece on it and sent it nationwide. Thus, the cat was completely out of the bag. My successor at *The Spectrum*, a Fargoan just back from Vietnam, Don Homuth, continued coverage of the upcoming event.[2]

---

1 "A Landing a Day: Zap, North Dakota," https://landingaday.wordpress.com/tag/zip-to-zap/.
2 Kevin Carvelle, letter to Robert Dodge, Nov 21, 2015.

When May 9 came, an estimated 3000 college students, some from distant states, descended on the town of Zap, with a population of 271, and the two local bars were soon dry. The following dawn 500 National Guardsmen entered the town with fixed bayonets and cleared out the drunken crowd. It was the only time in North Dakota history the National Guard was ever called out to control a riot,[1] and the Zip to Zap was the lead story that night on CBS News with Walter Cronkite,[2] as North Dakota State was widely publicized.

Steve Ward had joined the English Department by this time. He had started college at Stanford in 1956 and had some trouble, then dropped out. After being a farm laborer then a North Dakota lifeguard he had married and returned to school as an undergraduate at NDSU in 1960, then did his masters' degree in English. During that time, he took World Literature from Catherine, which he eventually ended up teaching, along with Catherine's former class, Humanities. He added, "I took Milton from her, of all things, because our Milton guy went away, ran away, or died, and Catherine, who could teach anything, took over the class."[3] After writing advertising and other work, he was hired in 1968 to join the English department, and was never made to feel second-class, or intimidated, because of having a master's degree and not a PhD, and stayed for 37 years.[4]

Of Catherine's general influence, he said, "She was a heck of a salesman for higher education. If going to college made Catherine 'Catherine,' then wow, I want some of that. So people wanted to be like Catherine. Nobody could, of course, but they wanted to go in that direction."[5] He also felt a personal debt that he described as, "I think before Catherine, I was afraid to say of myself, I was an intellectual. It sounded too high falootin.' After taking classes from Catherine, I was proud to say I was an intellectual. I always follow that up by saying I'm not very smart, but I am an intellectual. What does that mean? It means I love the

1 Chuck Haga, "Some Who Zipped to Zap Will Gather Again," Minnpost, https://www.minnpost.com/politics-policy/2009/05/some-who-zipped-zap-will-gather-again, May 5, 2009.
2 Ibid.
3 Steve Ward interview.
4 Ibid.
5 Ibid.

world of ideas. I got that from Catherine."[1]

During this time, the Tri-College University (TCU) came into existence that would bring new opportunities for Catherine. This was a consortium of North Dakota State University in Fargo, Moorhead State University, and Concordia College across the river in Moorhead, Minnesota, where students enrolled in one school could attend courses at the other two without additional tuition or fees.[2] The development of this arrangement had been in the works throughout the 1960s, and it was incorporated as a non-profit education corporation in 1970.[3] Greg Danz, who would become owner of Zanbroz Variety and Bookstore on Broadway in Fargo, had Catherine as a teacher in 1973 at the Tri-College University. He was in a seminar at Concordia College with five strong professors: Catherine, along with Delsie Holmquist, "Soc" Glasrud, and Drs. Anderson and Smerud of Concordia, and he wrote a paper on Hermann Hesse. Glasrud was his advisor and Catherine was on the panel evaluating his paper. He recalls, "All the professors were wonderful."[4] Another benefit of the Tri-College University came in 1972 with the National Endowment Grant for the Humanities of $400,000 that led to the establishment of the TCU Humanities Forum.[5] From that, Catherine and others established a major in humanities at NDSU.[6]

Catherine had also become involved in a community education program that offered classes without homework or grades, known as Communiversity. It originated in 1965, and was organized by Concordia College of Moorhead for the Fargo-Moorhead community, as Peggy Gaynor says, "to enrich the bleak, dark, cold days of February by having interesting courses and they would be offered on the weekend."[7] It was very successful and expanded to having classes all over town and all year long.

---

1 Ibid.
2 *Tri-College University*, https://www.tri-college.org/about_tcu/history_of_tcu/June10, 2013.
3 Ibid.
4 Greg Danz interview with Robert Dodge, Fargo, ND, October 14, 2015.
5 "Finding Aid to the Catherine Cater Papers," NDSU Archives, 3.
6 Ibid.
7 Peggy Gaynor interview.

Even 50 years after it had begun, and classes included wine tasting and food preparation, costs had only reached $12, with exceptions up to $55 for longer courses involving food and wine.[1] It managed to "pair the university and community and make for a sparkle in winter and it became a sparkle all year around."[2] Catherine was teaching two courses at Communiversity one year, one on the art of Jasper Johns, and she went right from that class to one on a popular novelist—Gaynor thinks it was John Grisham. That led her to comment, "I remember thinking, what kind of person is so comfortable in the world of ideas that she can dash from one venue in very interesting, but not easy art, then go to another on popular fiction and not miss a beat."[3]

In 1972, Catherine made her first appearance in the *Dictionary of American Scholars*, in the volume for English, Speech and Drama.[4] She was included in the next two editions that were released in 1978 and 1982. In 1975 she appeared in *Black Writers Past and Present: A Biographical Dictionary*[5]and ten years later *In Black and White*[6]included Catherine. *In Black and White* was a guide to magazine articles, newspaper articles, and books concerning Black individuals and groups. This was its third edition.

During this time Catherine's had her most difficult experience during her long career with the ACLU. She was a member of the National Advisory Council at the time when one of the most controversial decisions the organization faced was decided. It began in the summer of 1976 when Frank Collin, a member of George Lincoln Rockwell's Nazi Party of America, planned a demonstration in Chicago's Marquette Park. Chicago authorities said the park was booked, and police were instructed to ar-

---

1 Robin Huebner, "Communiversity Celebrates 50th Year of Learning, Fargo *Forum* online, http://www.inforum.com/news/education/3674565-communiversity-celebrates-50th-year-learning, Feb 8, 2015.
2 Peggy Gaynor interview.
3 Peggy Gaynor interview.
4 *Dictionary of American Scholars, Sixth Edition, Vol. 2: English, Speech, & Drama* (New York: R.R. Bowker, 1974).
5 Theressa Gunnels Rush, Carol Fairbanks Myers, and Esther Spring Arata, *Black American Writers Past and Present: A Biographical and Bibliographical Dictionary* (Metuchen, NJ: Scarecrow Press, 1975).
6 Mary Mace Spradling, ed, *In Black and White* (Detroit: Gale Research, 1985).

rest Collin if he said "anything derogatory."[1] He was arrested and acquitted, and then he requested a permit to march outside the city. The park district found a rarely used law and told Collin he would have to post a $350,000 bond before his march would be approved. The Nazis planned to march through Skokie, a Jewish area where ten percent of the residents were survivors of the concentration camps of the Holocaust.[2] Collin announced his plan on May 1, 1977 to stage a march in Nazi uniforms, displaying swastikas and distributing anti-Jewish literature through the village of Skokie. The village responded by filing a petition in Circuit Court of Cook County to prevent the march.

Collin and his NAZI colleagues contacted the Illinois branch of the ACLU for its support, alleging violation of their First Amendment rights of assembly and free speech, and the Illinois ACLU sided with him.[3] ACLU lawyer Burton Joseph, who would later defend demonstrators arrested in Chicago's 1968 Democratic National Convention, originally represented the NAZI plaintiffs.[4] The board of directors of the ACLU national office, which included Catherine, fully supported the position of the Illinois chapter.[5]

The Circuit Court issued an injunction that prohibited "[m]arching, walking or parading in the uniform of the National Socialist Party of America; [m]arching, walking or parading or otherwise displaying the swastika on or off their person; [d]istributing pamphlets or displaying any materials which incite or promote hatred against persons of Jewish faith or ancestry or hatred against persons of any faith or ancestry, race or religion."[6] The village passed ordinances requiring the $350,000 bond and requiring permits for demonstrations. Over 500,000 U.S. citizens signed petitions supporting Skokie's efforts to prevent the

---

1 William A. Donohue, *The Politics of the American Civil Liberties Union,* (Piscataway, NJ: Transaction Publishers, 1985), 254.
2 Ibid.
3 Ibid.
4 Daarel Burnette II, "Burton Joseph, 1930-2010: Attorney Championed Civil Rights," Chicago *Tribune,* Apr 1, 2001.
5 Irving Louis Horowitz and Victoria Curtis Bramson, "Skokie, the ACLU and the Endurance of Democratic Theory," *Law and Contemporary Problems,* Vol. 43, No. 2, Spring 1979, 331.
6 *National Socialist Party of America v. Village of Skokie,* 432 U.S. 43 (1977), 43.

NAZI demonstration from taking place.[1]

This injunction was upheld at the appellate level, and by the Illinois Supreme Court, which denied a stay, or stop, of the injunction, and refused an accelerated hearing. The ACLU next approached U.S. Supreme Court Justice John Paul Stevens for a stay of execution. He treated it as a petition of certiorari, so the full Court heard it. The decision of the Supreme Court came on June 14, 1977. In a *per curiam* or "by the court" opinion, the Supreme Court reversed the Illinois Supreme Court decision and remanded the case to Illinois for reconsideration. It was called "by the court" but there were four members who dissented.[2]

On its return to Illinois, the case began at the appellate level and the injunction was overturned and modified. The only restriction put on the march was that it not include the display of swastikas. This decision was again appealed to the Illinois Supreme Court. According to the facts, "plaintiff's complaint that the 'uniform of the National Socialist Party of America consists of the storm trooper uniform of the German Nazi Party embellished with the Nazi swastika'; that the plaintiff village has a population of about 70,000 persons of which approximately 40,500 persons are of 'Jewish religion or Jewish ancestry' and of this latter number 5,000 to 7,000 are survivors of German concentration camps; that the defendant organization is 'dedicated to the incitation of racial and religious hatred directed principally against individuals of Jewish faith or ancestry and non-Caucasians'; and that its members 'have patterned their conduct, their uniform, their slogan and their tactics along the pattern of the German Nazi Party.' "[3] Defendant Frank Collin, who said he was the "party leader" contended they planned a "peaceful public assembly," where "The marchers were to wear uniforms which include a swastika emblem or armband. They were to carry a party banner containing a swastika emblem and signs containing such statements as 'White Free Speech,' 'Free Speech for the White Man,' and 'Free Speech for White America.' The demonstrators would not distribute handbills, make any derogatory statements

---

1 Ian C. Friedman, *Freedom of Speech and the Press* (New York: Infobase Publishing, 2009), 75.
2 *National Socialist Party of America v. Village of Skokie*, 432 U.S. 43 (1977), 44.
3 *Village of Skokie v. National Socialist Party of America*, 69 Il. 605, 1978.

directed to any ethnic or religious group, or obstruct traffic."[1]

The Illinois Court's *per curiam* decision said, "The only issue remaining before this court is whether the circuit court order enjoining defendants from displaying the swastika violates the first amendment rights of those defendants."[2] Their ruling was, "the display of the swastika cannot be enjoined under the fighting-words exception to free speech, nor can anticipation of a hostile audience justify the prior restraint." [3] The Nazi march was still on.

Though the Nazis won their right to march in Skokie, they never did it.[4] The *California Law Review* wrote a rather supportive article on the position the ACLU had taken, concluding, "We find ourselves, after all, in the midst of history, inhabiting an enormous nation whose citizens frequently despise each other, and ruled by a government with several million armed men under its command and technology to turn any segment of humanity into a thin gas within the space of half an hour. It is in this setting, free speech as a right that actually works, that curbs the natural instinct of our citizens and our government to suppress the things that they do not want to hear."[5]

Many members of the ACLU registered their opinion on the organization's actions in this case by dropping out.[6] Nearly 20% of the organization's 250,000 members gave up their memberships in protest over its support of the Nazis.[7] Catherine had found it an extremely difficult position to be in, but she was one of those who voted to support the ACLU's actions, saying, "If you do not give the same rights to those to whom you do not agree with, that you give to those with whom you agree, then you are not in agreement with the ACLU."[8]

It would certainly be erroneous to believe that because of this, Catherine condoned, or was in any way accepting of bigots

---

1 Ibid.
2 Ibid.
3 Ibid.
4 Donohue, *The Politics of the American Civil Liberties Union*, 254-255.
5 Edward L. Rubin, "Review: Nazis, Skokie, and the First Amendment as Virtue," *California Law Review*, Vol. 74, No. 1, Jan 1986, 260.
6 Donohue, *The Politics of the American Civil Liberties Union*, 256.
7 Friedman, *Freedom of Speech and the Press*, 74.
8 Vanorny, interview of Catherine Cater, Tape B.

and bigotry. She believed in open discussion and celebrated free expression, but she was intolerant of intolerance, as her resignation from Olivet College demonstrated.

Catherine was selected to give the Faculty Lectureship Award Address in early 1982, and not surprisingly, she chose to speak on the power of myth, especially those that have come down from ancient Greece. The speech she gave offers insight into her as a teacher and scholar. The talk received surprisingly detailed coverage in the Fargo *Forum*.[1] She named her talk "Fire and Rock," and started with an introduction of a question basic to philosophy since Plato and Aristotle: where reality exists, in one's mind or externally. She began, "Centuries ago, a Chinese philosopher dreamed one night that he was a butterfly, fluttering about, enjoying himself. Upon awakening the next morning, he wondered whether he had dreamed he was a butterfly, or whether he was now a butterfly dreaming he was a man."[2] She said dreams tend to vanish unless they are repeated, but one kind of dream is valid for all people and that is myth. While myth can have several meanings, scholars explore them as shared dreams. "Myths can be described as narratives shared by cultures,"[3] and they are concerned with good and evil. She stated that a contemporary physicist identified science as "our new mythology" and "Unlike legends, myths deal, not with historical characters and events, but with realities perceived and shared by the culture out of which they have emerged."[4]

Catherine then discussed Prometheus, one of the most familiar of Greek myths, which had been transmitted orally and in print, sometimes in tone, with different details and narrative, but essentially the same story. Prometheus was a gigantic offspring of heaven and earth who created mortal man, and tried to outwit Zeus after his request for fire for his creation was turned down. Prometheus stole a spark from Mount Olympus, and bestowed it on man, bringing him fire. This earned a two-fold pun-

---

1 "NDSU Faculty Lecture Centers on Durable Myths," Fargo *Forum*, March 1, 1982, 4.
2 Catherine Cater, "Fire and Rock," 26th Faculty Lectureship Award Address, Feb 28, 1982, Box 1, File 34, Catherine Cater Collection, North Dakota State University Archives, Fargo, ND, 1.
3 Ibid.
4 Ibid.

ishment from Zeus, who created Pandora to plague man, and had Prometheus nailed to rock on Mount Caucasus. This was fire and rock, as Catherine called her speech. An eagle came daily and devoured the prisoner's liver, which grew back each night. After many years, the hero Heracles and the sacrificial death of a centaur managed the release of Prometheus.[1]

Myths surrounding Prometheus had fascinated writers and artists from ancient times through the present, she informed the audience, citing Aeschylus' *Prometheus Bound* in the 5th Century B.C. In her final words she related the myth of fire and rock to the Cold War as she said:

> Whatever the interpretation, critical or fictional, the Prometheus myth, like other myths, continues to capture imaginations and demand a reworking appropriate to the culture that takes the myth into itself. In the case of the Promethean myth, the symbols used are shared by cultures from throughout the world.
>
> Fire and rock have engaged cultures' attention worldwide. For the Jivaro Indians of Northern Peru a hummingbird brought fire to humankind, while in Hindu theology Lord Agni is god of fire and fire itself, his column of flame representing the world's axis.
>
> With rock or stone the creation of men from stones is common to mythology. A Melanesian myth describes the spontaneous eruption of man from stone. Sisyphus, a Greek king, angered Zeus and was condemned to roll a rock up a hill that would constantly roll back down on him. The French writer Camus saw the myth of Sisyphus as illustrating the human condition but speculates that in his ceaseless struggle Sisyphus might be happy. To Aeschylus, when Prometheus brought fire to men he brought civilization and advancement. To Buddhists it means wisdom, but fire also can bring destruction.
>
> Modern myths have their ground, then, in tension between the splintering and depersonalization of hu-

---

1 Ibid., 2.

man effort and in a quest for a center of being. A 20th century Irish poet writes of ages before ours but ex‑ presses eloquently a myth of our time:

> Things fall apart; the centre cannot hold;...
> The best lack all conviction, while the worst
> are full of passionate intensity.

Although Gilgamesh's search for immortality and Rama's heroic efforts to overcome illusion are no more alien to our time and place in the world than are other ancient mythical themes, these themes have been trans‑ formed to match the temper of an age in which compel‑ ling force lies in inconceivable consequences of our own creations.

It is not that the centre cannot hold; rather, it is that mythical themes of atomized survival and those of life with a centre have not yet been reconciled. The rock has been splintered and fire threatens to consume us, not save us.[1]

There was soon another attempt to solicit additional monies from Rueben Askanase at about this time that Jerry Richardson remembers well. The phone rang in his office in Ceres Hall on a Monday morning in 1984 and it was Askanase, who called him frequently. Acting President Bob Koob proposed that Richard‑ son convey the idea of another project to Askanase that would involve a contribution to NDSU.[2] Koob suggested that Askanase establish an honorary professorship in Catherine's name. Jerry presented the idea to Askanase, who asked him, "How much do you think that might cost?"[3]

After checking with Koob, Jerry told him, "half a million dollars."

Askanase responded, "That's way too much! What else can you suggest?"[4] The suggestion was for a series of prominent

---

1 Ibid., 2‑3.
2 Jerry Richardson interview and Jerry Richardson, "Dr. Catherine Cater & The Life of the Mind," unpublished at time of manuscript preparation.
3 Ibid., "Dr. Catherine Cater & The Life of the Mind".
4 Ibid.

guest lecturers, and Askanase was to set the amount of his do-nation for funding it at whatever level he felt comfortable with. Thus was born the Catherine Cater Humanities Lecture Series, and Catherine could select distinguished humanities educators to NDSU.[1]

The first speaker on the series was surprised to be chosen. It was October 1987 and Pat Stocker, better known to me as my sister, Patty Dodge Stocker, gave the lecture. At the time she was Associate Dean of the Business School at the University of Maryland. She recalls, "I have no idea why I was asked. I wasn't particularly prominent. But in any case, I did give the lecture and remember that I talked about *Death of a Salesman* in terms of its messages about business and ethics. I also emphasized something I have said more times than I can count, that the best education for students is a liberal arts undergraduate focus— then a career-oriented focus (e.g., law, business, medicine) at the graduate level. I recall she thanked me profusely at the end of my talk."[2]

In 1987, Catherine retired as a full time professor at NDSU, though she remained on as a teacher until the early in the twen-ty-first century, offering humanities seminars and individual study for students in the Scholars Program.[3] Peggy Gaynor, one of Catherine's close friend notes, "I don't think you could call what she did retiring, because she never lost touch with stu-dents or the things that mattered to her. But little by little she lived in her house more and on campus less. On the hottest day of the summer she'd have that straw hat with the nice big brim covering her face and she'd be walking over to campus."[4] Cath-erine's view was, "Now I have the best of all worlds because I don't have to go to meetings. I will concentrate on students."[5]

In the following years speakers on the Catherine Cater Lec-ture Series included University of Chicago President Hanna Gray, Steven Toulmin of Northwestern, Frederick Bernthal of the National Science Foundation, Bard College President Leon

---

1 Ibid.
2 Email Pat Stocker to Robert Dodge, Nov 16, 2015.
3 Email Thomas Riley to Robert Dodge, October 15, 2015.
4 Interview Peggy Gaynor.
5 "Excerpts: Catherine Cater," NDSU Magazine.

Botstein, Brown University President Vartan Gregorian, Yale historian Howard Lamar, Sheldon Hackney of the National Endowment for Humanities, psychologist Richard Voss, and North Dakota historian Clay Jenkinson, among others.[1] Don Larew, the design and technical theater director who came to NDSU in 1969, said, "Certainly the lecture series that she established, which was of a limited time, was of an extreme importance."[2]

Larew noted something else about Catherine, which was her support of the arts. He observed that she was always "very supportive of what we were doing in the theater," and saw her "as someone in our corner."[3]

Catherine expanded the arts at NDSU in other ways as well. In 1969 with her advice and urging, an art collection was begun for display at the Memorial Union that has continued to grow ever since.[4] Mike Morrissey's wife, Susan, was an artist, and Mike remarked, Catherine was always interested in Susan's art endeavors, would always show up at her openings, arrive by taxicab, get out sprightly. She was, he said, "As encouraging and supportive of Sue as she was to me."[5]

She was prominent and generous at cultural events throughout the community. Ene Vogel observed, "She attended so many community events, whether they were cultural, social service. In our small community there are lists of contributors to the art galleries, symphony, cultural activities, service organizations. I think Catherine's name appeared on just about all of those lists."[6]

---

1 Richardson, "Dr. Catherine Cater & The Life of the Mind."
2 Don Larew interview with Robert Dodge, Fargo ND, October 12, 2015.
3 Ibid.
4 "NDSU Shares Its Act Collection Via the Internet," https://www.ndsu.edu/news/banner_stories/digitalgallery/, Nov 14, 2013.
5 Mike Morrissey interview.
6 Ene Vogel interview.

CHAPTER 12. CATHERINE CATER AS YODA

Stephen Disrud is a lecturer in English as a Second Language at North Dakota State University. He took a course on Greco-Roman philosophy and a tutorial on esthetics from Catherine in the mid 1990s in the Scholars program, where Catherine continued teaching until 1998.[1] Disrud recalls the midterm exam's essay his class was given that he thought illustrated her teaching style and expectations. It was a two-and-a-half-hour exam, and the assignment was "Define Be." He explained, "There were no instructions, there were no requirements, there were no parameters, or any indication of her thinking on the topic. It was just 'Define Be.' Which threw me into a task that I didn't know I could accomplish until I accomplished it. I was thrown into a panic for a bit, but then proceeded to set out on it. I am now a teacher and I would never, ever consider doing that to a student, but she had a certain force of personality that made that work. You knew it was going to be productive, because she had a reputation that it had been productive for generations of students, so you just trusted her. She also had a certain force of character. She was the great Catherine Cater, and I don't know anyone else who could do it the way she could do it."[2]

---

1 Homan, "A Humanist in Honors," 89.
2 Stephen Disrud interview with Robert Dodge, Fargo, ND, October 13, 2015.

Disrud and his classmates came up with a name for Catherine that suited her well. He recalls, "We used to call her Yoda. She reminded us of Yoda. She had sort of the outsized features, but that really wasn't a race thing."[1] For those unfamiliar with the *Star Wars* films, Yoda was of an "unknown species," and a legendary Jedi Master, small, but wise and powerful. In *The Empire Strikes Back*, Yoda described himself with "Luminous being are we . . . not this crude matter."[2] Physically, Yoda had wispy white hair, receding to near baldness, pointed ears sticking straight out of a greenish head, large eyes with circles above, bags below, an age-lined face and receding chin with a small, button nose, wrinkled neck.[3] As Catherine aged and carried on, there are certainly similarities. While not a warrior, she was a crusader for equality and rights, and all agreed she was wise. She remained an "unknown species" throughout her Fargo years. It was possible to hear some of Catherine in Yoda, as when he said, "Fear is the path to the dark side... fear leads to anger...anger leads to hate...hate leads to suffering."[4]

Even her hair had similarities to Yoda's. Mike Morrissey recalled, "I think there was a point in time when her hair went to war with her. It started to recede then she would tie it up in certain ways, then it would be in a bandana affair."[5]

The question of her race made her an "unknown species" throughout her Fargo life. Morrissey said her African-American identity "Changed as the times changed. We could no longer pretend it didn't exist. She would vividly recount growing up where dogs were turned loose on demonstrating crowds, in Birmingham."[6] Thomas Riley, who was Dean of the College of Humanities and Social Studies until 1996 and knew Catherine for 15 years, wrote of initially being unaware that Catherine was African-American, though he thought she might be. He said he learned from Roland Dille, retired President of Moorhead State,

---

1 Ibid.
2 http://www.starwars.com/databank/yoda.
3 Ibid.
4 From *The Phantom Menace*, "Starwars.com 10: Best Yoda Quotes," *Star Wars*, http://www.starwars.com/news/the-starwars-com-10-best-yoda-quotes.
5 Mike Morrissey interview.
6 Ibid.

that Catherine suffered from vitiligo.[1] Vitiligo is a progressive condition involving loss of pigmentation in the skin. It can be disfiguring, and no effective cure or treatment exists.[2] The condition presents itself in loss of skin color in blotches,[3] with the most famous case being Michael Jackson. This seems an unlikely diagnosis for Catherine, who had light skin since college, according to published photographs, and she told Nancy Hanson in a 1983 interview that in seeking employment she could have "identified herself with the white majority in those communities because of her fair complexion. But she chose not to do so."[4] Perhaps vitiligo exacerbated things in some way, but it does not appear to be the cause of her appearance being indistinct. Her ambiguous appearance was evident when she visited Hong King and was touring with a Chinese group. The guide or the tour asked her, "What part of China are you from?"[5]

While her physical heritage was always a bit mysterious, she retained no trace of a Southern accent, which was noted by Ellen Kosse in the *Spectrum*. There, Catherine explained another of her qualities that was obvious to all who knew her. It was elegance, and Catherine filled out a definition of herself by explaining the word: "Elegance is a state of mind that rejects the shoddy and the cheap. It is hostile to both snobbery and pretense. I do believe very firmly elegance leads to an awareness that there are many more choices than on the surface."[6] She also spoke of coping with discrimination both as a member of a minority and as a woman, telling Kosse, "Perhaps the most difficult task facing individuals is to refuse to recognize condescension. Condescension can exist only if it is accepted."[7]

Paul Homan pointed out that "She had her own kind of style. It was a little bit of a different era. She had her own uniform. It

---

1 Thomas Riley Email to Robert Dodge, October 15, 2015.
2 Linda Papadopoulos, Robert Bor and Charles Legg, "Coping With the Disfiguring Effects of Vitiligo: A Preliminary Investigation into the Effects of Cognitive-Behavioural Therapy," *British Journal of Medical Psychology*, Vol. 72, 1999, 385.
3 "Diseases and conditions: Vitiligo, *Mayo Clinic*, http://www.mayoclinic.org/diseases-conditions/vitiligo/basics/definition/con-20032007.
4 Hanson interview, 24.
5 Vanorny, interview of Catherine Cater, Tape B.
6 Kosse, "Cater: 'infect one another with the desire to learn.' "
7 Ibid.

was her coats. We all recognized her by her coats. It was a dated look, but it was fine."[1] It was not surprising it was from a different era when he commented. She kept teaching until she was in her middle 80s, and Paul had come to know her in her later stages of life, though they were very close as educators and friends.

Another factor in Catherine's life was her close personal friendship with Delsie Holmquist. While they were colleagues for many years both at Moorhead State and NDSU, and designed courses on humanities together, they also shared a house and accompanied each other to cultural and intellectual events, as well as being traveling companions. It was a compatible relationship between two women who had few intellectual equals, enjoyed each other's company, and looked after each other.

While they were likeminded in many ways, their personalities differed. Steve Ward noted, "She [Delsie] was just like a bull. She was so strong and so forceful. Catherine was too, but in a much quieter way."[2]

In 1970, Delsie gave a speech honoring Catherine for the Blue Key Doctor of Service Award to the Blue Key fraternity at a banquet. She expressed her high regard for Catherine, first saying, "I find this an occasion that I cannot readily bypass."[3] The reason she couldn't pass up the chance to speak, she explained, was that it gave her an opportunity to voice publicly some of what she meant when she said to others, "Happiness is when one lives with said Catherine Cater."[4]

Catherine traveled extensively with Delsie. Catherine commented on their travel, saying, "I have found travel very restorative, indeed. One sees other people, other places that distract one from whatever problems one has."[5] Catherine described London is her all-time favorite destination. She singled out visits to the incomparable British Museum, specifying the letters of Robert Graves, an authority on Greek mythology, adding, "But there is never as much time as I'd like, only enough to view the

1 Paul Homan interview.
2 Steve Ward interview.
3 Delsie Holmquist, Speech about Catherine Cater to NDSU Blue Key Fraternity Banquet, 1.
4 Ibid.
5 "Excerpts: Catherine Cater".

Egyptian sculptures and the Elgin marbles."[1]

While Catherine studied in Ireland, France, England and Sweden, she traveled, usually with Delsie, through much of Europe, Hong Kong, China, the Soviet Union, Mexico, and Thailand, among other places.[2] Delsie commented on Catherine's travel habits, saying, "When she travels, she prepares. She studies the country, refreshes herself on the languages, pours over maps, and studies the history of the special places that she thinks will be fruitful to her purposes."[3]

A special trip was to the Turkish coast, the location of ancient Greek colonies including Miletus, which had special meaning to Catherine. This was the home of Thales, traditionally considered the first philosopher,[4] who sought a single underlying element as the basis for everything. It was also where the other Pre-Socratics of the sixth century B.C. lived: Anaximander and Anaximenes, who constructed theories about an underlying basis for the universe as a whole, and in the following century, Democritus and Anaxagoras who advanced new ideas of the nature of reality and how the universe functions. It was here that Zeno and his paradoxes introduced questions on the nature of reality and whether it was in what was observed or thought, paving the way for the Aristotle-Plato debate to follow. All was very familiar to Catherine, but to be there and walk where they once walked was a highlight for the longtime philosophy student and authority. Delsie shared Catherine's love of classical scholarship.

Catherine's race was a near anomaly and her attitudes on civil rights that she based on experience and philosophy were advanced for the Fargo-Moorhead Community. Yet she was such a special and recognizably superior individual, that the better choice was to learn from her rather than to consider questioning or challenging her. The community was fortunate to have her in its midst as all were elevated.

---

1 Nancy Hanson interview, 34.
2 *Finding Aid to the Catherine Cater Papers*: Biography, 3.
3 "Delsie Holmquist speech about Catherine Cater, to NDSU Blue Key Fraternity Banquet, for Blue Key Doctor of Service Award, 1970," 4.
4 *The Oxford Companion to Philosophy*, 869.

A notable Catherine quality was determination. She said, "I like obstacles,"[1] and told Nancy Hanson, "When I'm committed to a group, I'm really committed."[2] Peggy Gaynor recalled an example that described this quality in Catherine. "She had walked herself downtown one summer day, she was en route to the Fargo Theater to see a film and in the block in front of St. Mary's Cathedral she stumbled on the sidewalk and fell. She got herself up and dusted herself off. Her wrist hurt and she said, 'I didn't want to miss the movie.' She didn't go to have an X-ray until after she saw the movie and it turned out she had a broken wrist. She's a person who can set a goal and be quite true to it."[3]

Another admirable trait was Catherine's ability to easily mingle with people of any age. This was noted by Ene Vogel, who said, "Catherine had friends in all age groups. The years she joined the Vogel family for Thanksgiving dinners she could visit easily with our young son David, or with people who were young adults or middle aged. She just had a wonderful rapport with people of all ages."[4] Mike Morrissey made a similar observation, "How interestingly she could draw complete strangers into a table conversation that would last an evening—it was amazing, just amazing."[5]

Steve Ward expressed a way of viewing Catherine as Yoda, the small and wise member of an unknown species. His observation was, "She brought a broader perspective on human potential to the department, to the university, to Fargo and to North Dakota than we had experienced to that point. That was what was amazing about Catherine. She introduced us to things we had never thought about and we gained experience."[6] Mike Morrissey had a similar sentiment: "I always thought the cognoscenti,[7] if you will, of this community always looked to Catherine as a beacon of important ideas, different ways of thinking, cultural matters, racial matters."[8]

1 "Excerpts: Catherine Cater."
2 Hanson, "Catherine Cater," 34.
3 Peggy Gaynor interview.
4 Ene Vogel interview.
5 Mike Morrissey interview.
6 Steve Ward interview.
7 Intelligentsia, intellectuals
8 Mike Morrissey interview.

Of course, her most notable and obvious quality was her inquiring and always questioning mind. That was also her gift to all of us who were fortunate enough to have been her students or to have known her.

CHAPTER 13. CONTINUITY AND CHANGES

Delsie died on December 9, 1990, at age 92.[1] Her passing was a great loss to Catherine, as she had lost her longtime housemate, soul mate, traveling companion and intellectual companion. However one characterizes their relationship, they had a strong bond of interests and friendship and had relied on each other for mutual support. Catherine remained in the house on 10th Street North that was filled with 10,000 books piled on shelves and filling the garage.

Delsie left a large amount of money to North Dakota State University, dedicated to Catherine, and none to Moorhead State University.[2] Yvonne Condell said Don Larew had told her Delsie left the money to NDSU for scholarships, and she looked in the Moorhead State brochure and found that Delsie had left nothing for that institution. She said, "I don't know if that was Catherine's influence or what it was. That troubles me."[3] What upset her was that Delsie had been at Moorhead State for 37 years, much longer than her NDSU career, and according to Condell, the donation she made was the "largest amount given at that time."[4] Dr. Condell's protective attitude about Moorhead State is understandable, given

---

1   U.S. Social Security Death Index.
2 Don Larew interview.
3 Yvonne Condell interview.
4 Ibid.

her significance to the institution, and higher education expenses and struggles for funding by reaching out to donors to enhance programs. Still, it was Delsie's money, and her bond with Catherine makes it unsurprising that this would have been her choice.

Catherine continued teaching the "Third Year Seminar," the course students took before their senior project in the Scholars Program.[1]

That fall the Bison had won the NCAA Division II football championship with a 51–11 victory over Indiana University of Pennsylvania.[2] It is doubtful that this brought much joy to Catherine. She had said back in 1977 when the football program had grown large that she saw a conflict between academic and athletic facilities on campus. She referred to what was then the new Fieldhouse as the "the mausoleum at the end of the campus,"[3] and expressed disappointment that NDSU was being judged for what it had physically, not academically.[4]

During these years Kathleen Weir, commonly known as Kathy, was a successful attorney for Gunhus, Grinnell, Klinger Swenson & Guy in Moorhead, Minnesota. She was divorced[5] and had a large home in Moorhead where she often entertained and invited faculty members from Moorhead State and NDSU.[6] This may have been where she and Catherine became acquainted.[7] Kathy Weir was appointed to the position of Clay County Minnesota District Court Judge in the late 1980s.

In the year 2000 Catherine donated a lifetime collection of souvenirs from her travels and family heirlooms in hopes to raise money for a lecture series. "We would like to attract people who can contribute to the thinking of students—challenging students to think about ideas and values outside their immediate experience,"[8] said Catherine. Peggy Gaynor bought a small dish

1 Paul Homan interview.
2 "1990 NCAA Division II Football National Championship Game," *The Official Site of North Dakota State*, http://www.gobison.com/sports/1990/12/8/757313132.aspx?id=1718.
3 Kosse, "Cater: 'infect one another with the desire to learn...'"
4 Ibid.
5 *Minnesota Statewide Divorce Index, 1970-1995*, St Paul, MN, USA: Minnesota Department of Health.
6 Peggy Gaynor interview.
7 Ibid.
8 "Souvenirs Donated to NDSU," Grand Forks *Herald* (ND), November

of Catherine's that reminded her of her youth. She still uses it for olives or nuts, and "every time I take it down I think of Catherine and the richness of her life and the richness of my life for having Catherine in it."[1] The hope in the sale of these collectables was to revive the Catherine Cater Lecture Series that had begun in 1987. Catherine's donations raised $8,000, and another $2,500 came in donations,[2] but the lecture series was not restored.

Kathy Weir and Catherine became good friends. Catherine was getting older, but no less wise and still an eager learner. I visited Fargo some time after the 9/11 attack in 2001 and we had lunch at the Radisson Hotel. I was teaching a philosophy course at the time and she suggested ways for me to introduce Descartes to students. What surprised me most was when she mentioned that she was learning Arabic, since she thought it was an important language to understand. Ene Vogel had a similar experience with Catherine that she passed on. She related, "Catherine was the epitome of a lifelong learner. Education was something you didn't ever finish. Just to prove the point. This was, she was older, in her 80s. We had invited Catherine to a get together with women friends we were having over to say goodbye to our friend, Nancy Brodie, who was moving out East. Catherine was invited and she was enthusiastic, as she always was, to accept the invitation. But she said, 'I have Arabic class. Would you mind if I got there a little bit late?' And sure enough, she came a bit late with her book bag and notes from her Arabic lesson and joined right into the activities. Catherine squeezed a lot of learning and a lot of friendships into her life."[3]

Catherine attended a reception at the gallery in the Fine Arts Building and was introduced to Lourdes Hawley who worked as a graphic artist in the NDSU publications office. Catherine said, "I already know you."[4] Hawley's husband was an instructor in the Modern Language Department, which had taken control of the Scholars Program. Catherine and Lourdes became friends and talked, not about what Lourdes was doing, but her ideas.

19, 2000, 7.
1 Peggy Gaynor interview.
2 Associated Press, Grand Forks *Herald* (ND), November 20, 2000, 7.
3 Ene Vogel interview.
4 Lourdes Hawley telephone interview with Robert Dodge, November 25, 2015.

She was an artist also, and Catherine was drawn to artists. Lourdes watched Catherine walk away from the gallery and put on her floppy straw hat and sunglasses. She was captivated by the image as well as by Catherine, who "was what she hoped she would be when she grew to be that age."[1] She got an image of Catherine from the publications department and had and enlarged it to 23 by 26 inches, covered it with beeswax, colored it with pastels[2] and added Catherine's floppy hat. She called it "When I Grow Up."

The Memorial Union Gallery, where this is displayed, posted this comment about Catherine and the work of art on its Facebook page:

> Catherine Cater was a lifelong supporter of NDSU students and the Memorial Union Gallery. Dr. Cater was influential in creating the Student Art Selection Committee at NDSU, and the pieces this committee purchased form the foundation of our Student Art Collection. We will forever be grateful for the legacy Dr. Cater created at NDSU.
>
> In her honor, "When I Grow Up. . . ," a drawing of Catherine Cater by Lourdes Hawley, is on view in the Memorial Union Gallery.[3]

The image is on the cover of this book.

Catherine's teaching career finally came to an end. Shortly before, she was awarded an honorary Doctor of Fine Arts diploma by NDSU in 2001 in recognition of her dedication to teaching and promotion of the humanities.[4] In a speech for an unnamed event that Catherine titled "Yet Generations Remain the Same,"[5] she outlined major forces that had affected her career. She wrote that she was about to begin her 55th year of teaching, and began

1 Ibid.

2 Memorial Union Gallery Collections, Object ID: M159, www.ndsu.edu/mu/programs/gallery/collections/.

3 "Catherine Cater," Memorial Union Gallery (NDSU) Facebook Page, August 13, 2015.

4 "Finding Aid to the Catherine Cater Papers," Biography, 2.

5 Catherine Cater, "Yet Generations Remain the Same," Box 1, File 35, Catherine Cater Collection, North Dakota State University Archives, Fargo, ND.

by explaining that she would explore three societal movements that had affected her: war, anti-Communism, and the third was difficult to sort out, but it involved the growing emphasis on technology, economic security, and multiculturalism. She first discussed her Olivet College experience with the Red Scare and how "Students from the University of Chicago joined the protest while Norman Thomas, standing under a large oak tree, orated on democratic freedoms."[1] Also under attack were readings such as Ruth Benedict's *Patterns of Culture*, Margaret Mead's *Coming of Age in Samoa*. When not picketing or writing letters, students carried on with classes and related their latest experiences to the material. She concluded, "I believe that the students, my colleagues, and I learned much about social interaction and about people's anxieties, beliefs, assumptions, and motivations."[2] From that she moved to what was then the present with, "Today many of us have distance from the physical conflicts in the Middle East, Korea, Bosnia, Ireland, and elsewhere. A democracy is, however, never free of psychological and social conflict—probably the human animal never is."[3] Her final point was to express a degree of frustration with the changing world. She observed, "Perhaps technology, the media, a kind of nervously frenetic pace of life have led some students to become impatient with the sounds of words, with readings that are 'too wordy,' or 'too hard,' or with that which has no immediate 'usefulness,' with thoughts that demand time for consideration of their intricacies."[4]

Just as Catherine was retiring, Kathy Weir had served as the Clay County judge for about 17 years and was given the opportunity to go to Kosovo to help with the ethnic violence following the breakup of Yugoslavia. She took a year's leave of absence from her job as County Judge in 2004, and then stayed for three years. In total, she spent five years in Kosovo, working as a trial judge and as a member of the Kosovo Supreme Court. Her summary of the experience was, "It was just overwhelming. To me, there was a real need for consistency."[5] She was assigned body-

---

1 Ibid., 4.
2 Ibid., 5.
3 Ibid.
4 Ibid.
5 Kathy Weir, quoted in Dave Olson, "Former Clay County Judge Helps Rebuild Justice in Kosovo," Fargo *Forum* online, April 12, 2010.

guards because her life was considered at risk. She presided over a number of war crimes trials in what was a conflict filled with atrocities. What she learned from the experience was, "We need to strive very, very hard—always—to protect out Bill of Rights so that we do not end up with the kind of oppression that happened in Kosovo."[1]

Greg Danz, who had lived in the area in the 1970s, returned to Fargo in 2009 and opened his business, Zanbroz, said Catherine was one of first people who came into his store. He "had the pleasure of having her as a customer and a book buyer her at the store for many years."[2] He noted, "When Katherine Weir was in Kosovo, she was concerned and interested in learning about the situation and keeping up with what was happening."[3]

Catherine continued to remain active in the community as a Fargo *Forum* article from 2005 notes. She was speaking at the Plains Art museum at a meeting of Philosophy for All on the topic, "How Free Are We?"[4] She liked introducing topics with questions for stimulating discussion.

Kathy and Catherine went to Mexico City to visit Kathy Weir's son and his Mexican wife.[5] While they were there, Catherine had a heart attack. Kathy arranged for a Lear jet to return Catherine to Fargo where she could receive good care.[6] Kathy lived with Catherine in her 10th Street North house and became her very admirable caregiver. They redid the house to make it accessible for Catherine, and Kathy made sure she got to medical appointments, ate the right foods, took her medicine at the right times. Kathy was an outstanding cook, so she prepared many things not only for Catherine and herself, but also for the many guests who came to visit as well. Stephen Disrud speaks of visiting, "More of a student coming to pay homage."[7] I visited on the two occasions I was in Fargo while Catherine was confined

---

1 Ibid.
2 Greg Danz interview.
3 Ibid.
4 "Best Bests," Philosophy for All, Plains Art Museum, Fargo. "How Free Are We?" presentation by Catherine Cater, followed by discussion, news@inforum.com, Sep 15, 2005.
5 Yvonne Condell interview.
6 Lou and Jerry Richardson interview.
7 Stephen Disrud interview.

to lying on her couch. Though restricted, her conversation was still exciting and her smile continuous, even while she had little strength in her emaciated body. Kathy found a watch for Catherine that had an alarm that would go off repeatedly during the day to announce that it was time for more pills, so she did not always need to be continually present.

This situation worked, but was very demanding for Kathy. Lou Richardson suggests, "At some point Kathy liked to travel and she didn't want to leave Catherine alone, and that's when they got her a room at Bethany. I think Catherine always thought of her house as her home and this was sort of her pied-à-terre or something. Her home away from home or something." Catherine took an independent living unit in Bethany Towers retirement home. Her Bethany Towers room was unlike any other I've ever seen. It appeared more like an office than a retirement living residence, with a large oval mahogany desk taking up much of the floor space and three computer terminals set out in different locations. She had a magnifying lens that slanted between her and the terminal on her desk, as her eyesight had deteriorated, but reading remained her essential pastime.

Author with Catherine at book signing, Fargo Library, September 2009

A major concern of hers during my first visit was her effort to sell her collection of 10,000 books. She maintained a considerable number of books in her Bethany residence and returned to her north side home to exchange them from time to time. She would also sleep at her old home on occasion after she first moved to the retirement residence.

Old friends visited regularly. Peggy Graynor recalls, "In the last few years I did volunteer work, so I had ample opportunity to be at Bethany. I would visit occasionally. She liked to have an appointment made for a visit rather than just dropping in."[1] She often visited with Don Larue both at Catherine's home and at Bethany.

Like Peggy, I would schedule my visits, usually by email since I was coming from overseas. My wife and I had left Fargo in 1979 and been overseas teachers in London then Singapore until 2014, and spent summers mainly in Colorado, but I still visited Fargo many summers for a brief stay to do banking and see old friends. Catherine and I exchanged email from time to time, and when I knew I would be in Fargo we would arrange a time for me to visit or to meet for lunch. This had also involved going out to dinner with the Vogels several times, and in 2009 Catherine came to a book launch I had at the Fargo Public Library, where I spoke about a book I had dedicated to her with, "To Catherine Cater for the privilege of having been your student."[2]

Once Catherine was in Bethany, we no longer met downtown for lunches. When I arrived she would be waiting for me outside at the door of the retirement facility. On occasions where friends dropped me off, she invited them up and was eager to get to know them. I spent hours with her in her room, talking and eating almonds. She always first inquired about my wife and daughter and my sister, then told me about Mike Morrissey, asked about the Vogels, and we discussed others we knew in common, then the conversation wandered in all directions. Catherine took considerable interest in my visits to leprosy victims in Singapore and frequently encouraged me to be writing about them and their experiences, which seemed unsurprising, given her concern for equal treatment for all. Also not

1 Peggy Gaynor interview.
2 *Prairie Murders*, North Star Press (St. Cloud, MN: 2009).

surprising, she quickly learned the names of other residents in the retirement home and greeted them warmly. They were very welcoming and friendly to her, and it was apparent that they enjoyed her company. The residents referred to her as "professor," and on several occasions when we were in the entryway or the dining room, people said, "The professor has a boyfriend," which I felt was a compliment even if it was a joke.

She was still "the professor" well into her 90s, and there were employees at Bethany who took advantage of it. She helped several who were NDSU students with their homework, including one who was studying bio-ethics.[1]

She always had the beliefs that had governed her life, and told me of how she dealt with the intolerant attitudes she encountered among some of the residents. It was still Catherine being Catherine, as she once said, "Another reason is that I came to believe that the best way to change the world is not to put Band-Aids on people's problems, but to educate them to make better decisions on their own."[2] Her way of educating people at the Bethany retirement home who were intolerant of Muslims and other non-Christian religions was to tell them that when she first came to the area, she had heard stories about the Ku Klux Klan burning crosses on the lawns of Catholics in Fargo. Intolerance of people whose beliefs were not identical to one's own was not only about people from far off places or with different sounding names, but could happen right here in Fargo when people would only welcome their own point of view.

Fact-checking Catherine is rather presumptuous, and of course her story was correct. The Fargo *Forum* in 1925, a little over 20 years before she arrived in the area, reported:

> Wearing their white robes and hoods, but with faces uncovered as required by North Dakota state law, the Ku Klux Klan paraded the streets of Fargo last night, as the feature event of the North Dakota state konklave, which opened yesterday morning. Between 750 and 800 were in the line of the march, including some 50 women, a 36-piece band and an 18 piece drum

1 Paul Homan interview.
2 Edmonds Hanson, "Catherine Cater," 20.

corps and also including 30 robed children in the 'junior Klan' riding on a float.[1]

Another visit brought out more typical Catherine. She had a limited number of books by her standards. Mike Morrissey observed, "Whether she was living alone or at Bethany the books were stacked in piles where she could grab the one that intrigued her at the moment."[2] I noticed an exceptionally large one and it was the ponderous *Oxford Classical Dictionary*,[3] nearly 2000 pages of Greek and Roman scholarship edited by Simon Hornblower. I told Catherine of my experience with Hornblower in a seminar during a course at Oxford called "New Directions in the Ancient World." It was a refresher for Classics and Ancient History teachers in England, taught by the leading authorities from the different Oxford colleges during the time my wife and I were teachers in London. The course was held in Corpus Christi College and all in attendance were Classics graduates of either Oxford or Cambridge, along with one graduate of NDSU. The handouts we were given in Greek and Latin, and were both literally and figuratively Greek to me. I told Catherine about Hornblower, who would take continuous questions on diverse topics in our seminar, and answer each with citations for articles to read, naming the journals, the issues, the dates and very often the page numbers. It was the most impressive display of memory I had ever seen, since these were random questions. It was understandable to me why he was editor of the massive *Oxford Classical Dictionary*. Catherine was interested and amused.

She then told me about her visit to Oxford. She apparently knew the instructor of the class she visited. She said she observed that the man grew frustrated when he continued with his class and received little reaction from the students. Eventually he invited Catherine to the front and asked her to speak. She said she started by asking questions and the students responded. Soon everyone was competing to get involved in the discussion as she took over the class. I'm sure she responded to

1 "8,000 Attend Celebration As Klansman Put on Rites, The Fargo *Forum*, Sept 20, 1925, 4
2 Mike Morrissey interview.
3 Simon Hornblower, *The Oxford Classical Dictionary* (Oxford, UK: 2005).

each comment with "Good!" and "What an excellent point!" as she validated everyone and related their comments to the great thinkers of all time. What worked with those of us in Fargo at NDSU with limited backgrounds worked as well at Oxford with students who were much better prepared.

Perhaps nothing says more about Catherine and what Jerry Richardson calls "the life of the mind"[1] than when I visited her in 2014 she introduced me to the online courses she was taking as she sat at her computer terminal and wanted to learn more. Paul Homan noted that in Catherine's later years, she was "always interested in a lot of things. If anything they broadened because she had a lot of time."[2]

Author with Catherine a month before her death

Summer was about to begin when I visited the next year. She was 98 and surprised me when she announced that she had become a fan of watching *Law & Order* on TV. What came as less of a surprise was that Catherine was taking an online course on the brain from MIT to better understand neurology. Her thirst for understanding and wisdom was unquenchable. Lou and Jerry Richardson also stopped in during that afternoon of June 11, 2015. It had been a different visit, with Catherine making frequent references to her age, and then showing the photos of her family that had previously been a mystery for her entire stay in the Fargo-Moorhead area. I remained and had dinner with her in the dining room at Bethany, then said goodbye. She seemed so healthy and vital, completely sharp mentally as always, and

1 Jerry Richardson interview.
2 Paul Homan interview.

walking comfortably. I thought it was likely I would return in the fall, so I told Catherine I would see her again soon.

It was a shock to hear the next month that the goodbye had been a final one. It was also the final time the Richardsons saw Catherine. Lou said, "She seemed totally healthy. I thought we had many visits ahead of us."[1] I heard that she died comfortably of pneumonia, what my mother used to call "the old people's friend."

1 Lou Richardson interview.

CHAPTER 14. THE LEGACY OF A TEACHER

Many have spoken about Catherine's legacy and the person she was, what made her so special to those who knew her and to NDSU. While she asked to go quietly and there were no ceremonies to celebrate her life at her passing, going quietly cannot be confused with being forgotten. Yvonne Condell expressed disappointment at Catherine's personal obituary, commenting, "I think for all the students she had, she owed them more than that little announcement in the paper. That was my feeling about it. All the people that held her in such high esteem: for them I felt there had to be some closure. I didn't think that statement she made was a closure. Maybe it was. I don't know."[1] Perhaps Yvonne is being unfair, but there is little doubt that Catherine was very important to many people and to North Dakota State University and that has been expressed frequently. Catherine's colleague Bill Cosgrove's statement had, to use a Catherine phrase, "shades of" the same thought. He wrote, "She was so knowledgeable herself and so instrumental in encouraging and contributing to knowledge in others, it seems a shame that she didn't allow people who loved and respected her so much to know more about her."[2]

North Dakota State University President Dean L. Bresciani

1 Yvonne Condell interview.
2 Bill Cosgrove Email.

spoke of Catherine in his State of the University Address during 2015's Homecoming. His words were, "I would like to take a moment to acknowledge the death of the legendary Catherine Cater this past summer. Many of you knew Catherine better than I did, but I particularly enjoyed a recent visit with her, as she recalled her experiences over her 50-plus years with NDSU students. She exuded an inner strength and displayed an incredible sense of humor and joy of life, and had a wonderful way of making you feel like a better person for being around her. I look forward to in the future announcing a permanent recognition of her impact on our campus community."[1] His comment that she "had a wonderful way of making you feel like a better person for being around her" captured something basic about knowing Catherine. Laura McDaniel, Associate Vice President for University Relations expressed a similar sentiment.[2]

Catherine's close personal friends offered their views, including Stephen Disrud who noted, "There isn't a Catherine Cater Library, there isn't a chair of philosophy that's endowed for Catherine Cater. I think in some ways there isn't a great legacy left at NDSU, which is regrettable. But at the time I think she touched a lot of people individually and I think she embodied something very important. So the impact, I don't know how you measure that. I think it's regrettably too little in the university."[3] Perhaps his call for more will be answered by the future gesture that Bresciani announced.

Catherine touching people individually, as Disrud mentioned, is a recurring theme. He specified, "I think she had a profound impact on individuals. I think she embodied certain values of the humanities. She was highly respected at NDSU, and we don't really have a figure on campus any more that represents all those classical values like she did."[4] Paul Homan observed, "Catherine's impact was on individuals, not institutions. She was not an institution-oriented person. The fact we have an honors program is an impact. It's her impact on people. In-

1 North Dakota State University State of the University Address, 2015, Fargo, https://www.ndsu.edu/president/speeches/stateoftheuniversityaddress2015/, October 8, 2015.
2 Laura McDaniel, Email to Robert Dodge, Oct 13, 2015.
3 Stephen Disrud interview.
4 Ibid.

dividuals. That was the beginning of it and the end of it. That's saying a lot."[1]

Ene Vogel commented, supporting Homan's statement with, "I was really thankful to have someone who was inspirational. It's amazing how she remembered all her students and was always reaching out. I really marvel at that. She had a genuine interest in people, and I think that's quite remarkable."[2] Steve Ward added, "She convinced a lot of us to teach. Did that to a lot of her students. Teaching is a great thing to do."[3] Pat Stocker was another of those impacted individuals, writing, "Perhaps what I loved most about Catherine was her constant inquisitiveness, her passion for learning new things. She absolutely twinkled when she would describe a book she had just read, described a course she was taking, or reflected on a conversation she had. This was particularly true during the last years of her life when many people are put off by the new technology they need to learn to fully participate in coursework, when they rest on their earlier successes, and when they feel it's really too much trouble to try something new. That wasn't Catherine! I also loved my visits with her—and I hope to live the rest of my life following that good example."[4]

Don Larew's observation about Catherine was, "I think there was a great impact. I think she influenced a large number of students. And not only those who were directly in her classroom. The Scholars Program was an important part of the program that she and Paul worked with and they brought that into the theater, so they brought that into our building, which helped us, in terms of having that level of intellect as well."[5] Thomas Riley who became Dean of the College of Humanities and Social Sciences in 1996 and had regular contact with Catherine for the next 15 years as dean and infrequent contact following that, wrote that "She was a gem here, and she was a good part of the glue that kept this campus together in the years before we as-

1 Paul Homan interview.
2 Ene Vogel interview.
3 Steve War interview.
4 Pat Stocker Email.
5 Don Larew interview.

pired to be a national presence in Higher Education."[1]

Letters to the Fargo *Forum* also reflected Catherine's lasting personal influence. Merle Johnson of Moorhead wrote, "Not only did she inculcate Socratic methodology with lasting impact on her students but did so in meaningful, understandable terms. She gave her students a utilitarian process for reasoning and for drawing sound conclusions that would last a lifetime."[2]

Gene Pinkney of Wahpeton, North Dakota, wrote extensively and with glowing praise, and awareness of Catherine's secret, "One professor, not a part of the English Department, still shines out first magnitude—my philosophy teacher, Dr. Cater. It was she who did most in those early pre-graduate years to teach us how to think.

"Time after time, her searching questions and perplexing paradoxes presented in the best Socratic style, sent me scurrying to the stacks looking for proofs to support assumptions I thought were valid. Her class should have been called the challenge of ideas, and she presented those challenges with an eloquence and kindness that prompted even some of the shyest students to venture opinions without fear of being scorned. She made Socrates and Plato come alive, and kids sat in the union talking philosophy, not rock and roll . . . And so, sweet Catherine, always so modest and self-effacing, always so gracious and kind, I hope one of your close friends someday writes the story of your exemplary life. The world deserves, nay needs to know that great ones such as yourself, who endured it all during times when being black made one a target for derision or even bullets, still emerged victorious."[3] Hopefully this book will respond in some way to Mr. Pinkney's wishes.

Kevin Carvelle expressed a similar sentiment with, "She absolutely deserves to be better known for she was an extraordinary light in Fargo Moorhead."[4]

---

1 Thomas Riley Email to Robert Dodge, October 15, 2015.
2 Merle Johnson, Letter," Wonderful Memories of Great Teachers," Fargo *Forum*, Sept 11, 2015.
3 Gene P. Pinkney, Letter, She Was a Brilliant Teacher Who Taught Us How to Think," Fargo *Forum*, Aug 23, 2015.
4 Carvelle, letter.

Other reflections are not of Catherine's legacy, but of Catherine the person and teacher, though where the dividing line is cannot be easily discerned. Peggy Gaynor's comment was, "If anybody ever encouraged people, she did it in a most unique way, a soft spoken way. But you wouldn't mistake soft spoken for being uncertain. She knew what she believed, she shared what she knew, she was passionate about education. She loved learning."[1] To Jerry Richardson, Catherine was "The life of the mind. When I think about Catherine Cater that was the thing that was so very important to her. What your mind was capable of being was at the root of all these things like the Scholars Program. If you're going to teach university students, that's what you're after, to teach them how to use your mind. The life of the mind is the phrase I would use to describe her."[2]

Steve Ward's description of Catherine is a slightly different take, but captures her accurately. He said, "She was like Socrates, only kinder. Socrates would end up pointing out to people how wrong they were, how dumb they were. Catherine never did that. Although, if you would listen to her and the allusions she made, you would realize by the end of the hour that you didn't know very much. And that was one thing that irritated me. I thought her major lesson was: 'You don't know very much, Steve.' I already knew that. I had the grades to show that."[3] He added, "It was just love of students and love of learning, and she put the two together. You can't beat that."[4]

Catherine Cater was the Socrates of NDSU and her lasting legacy of students who learned to ask questions rather than accept things without critical analysis remains valuable to every generation she taught. She was without equal in doing this with grace and elegance, and her willingness to listen carefully to oth-

1 Peggy Gaynor interview.
2 Jerry Richardson interview.
3 Steve Ward interview.
4 Ibid.

ers. The Scholars Program she initiated carries on that process to the credit of the university. The mystique she cultivated to obscure a painful past did nothing to diminish her infectious personality and the superior mind that did much to uplift the intellectual, artistic levels and concern for society at North Dakota State University and in the Fargo-Moorhead Community.

SOURCES

"25 Great Scholarships for African American Students: MSU Moorhead James & Yvonne Condell Endowed Scholarship," http://www.top10onlinecolleges.org/scholarships-for/african-american-students/.

1900 - History - U.S. Census Bureau - Census.gov. https://www.census.gov/history/www/through_the_decades/index_of_questions/1900_1.html.

"1960s Timeline." University Archives, Minnesota State University Moorhead. https://www.mnstate.edu/university-archives/125th-anniversary/1960s/ .

"1990 NCAA Division II Football National Championship Game." *The Official Site of North Dakota State.* http://www.gobison.com/sports/1990/12/8/757313132.aspx?id-1718 .

1993-2002 White Pages. Acxiom Corporation, Little Rock, AR. *Fargo*; State: *North Dakota*; Year(s): 1993, 1994, 1995.

"8,000 Attend Celebration As Klansman Put on Rites." The Fargo *Forum.* September 20, 1925.

"The African Slave Trade and the Middle Passage." *PBS.* http://www.pbs.org/wgbh/aia/part1/1narr4.html .

Alabama 1867 Voter Registration Records Database. Alabama Department of Archives and History. Montgomery, Alabama.

Alexander, Rev. W. S. "The Freedmen: Straight University: New Orleans, Louisiana," *American Missionary.* 32, Iss. 6, June 1878.

Allen, Glen O. "The Fall of Endymion: A Study in Keats's Intellectual Growth," *Keats–Shelley Journal.* Winter 1957.

"Along the Color Line." *The Crisis.* 3, No. 4, February 1912.

Anderson, Albert. "Steady Growth: 60 Race Teachers In White Colleges." *Pittsburgh Courier*, February 1, 1947.

The Annual Register of the University of Chicago, 1915–1916. Chicago: The University of Chicago Press, September 1916.

"Askanase, Reuben W." *Texas State Historical Association*. https://tshaonline. org/handbook/online/articles/fasph.

Associated Press. Catherine Cater auction, Grand Forks *Herald* (ND). November 20, 2000.

The Atlanta University Bulletin. The Catalogue 1911-1912, Atlanta: Atlanta University, *Atlanta University Catalogs*. Book 42. s. II http://digitalcommons. auctr.edu/aucatalogs/42 .

Banks, Adelle M. "Rev. Ralph Abernathy: Martin Luther King, Jr.'s Overlooked 'Civil Rights Twin.'" *Huffington Post*, November 20, 2015, http:// www.huffingtonpost.com/2015/01/19/rev-ralph-abernathy-civil-rights_n_6482176.html .

Bardaglio, Peter W. "Rape and the Law in the Old South: 'Calculated to excite Indignation in every heart.' " *The Journal of Southern History*, 60, No. 4, November, 1994.

"Baseball's Joe DiMaggio Dies at 84," Los Angeles *Times*, March 9, 1999.

Bass, Eric Z. "The Strange Life of Strange Fruit." *Deep South* Magazine online, http://deepsouthmag.com/2012/the-strange-life-of-strange-fruit/, December 12, 2012

Bates, Beth Tompkins. *Pullman Porters and the Rise of Protest Politics in Black America, 1925-1945*. Chapel Hill, NC: The University of North Carolina Press, 2001.

Bearak, Barry. "Where Football and Higher Education Mix." New York *Times*, September 17, 2011.

Berry, Daina. *Swing the Sickle for the Harvest is Ripe: Gender and Slavery in Antebellum Georgia*. Champaign, Ill: University of Illinois Press, 2007.

"Best Bests." Fargo *Forum*. September 15, 2005.

Best, Wallace. "Politics and the Misuse of Langston Hughes," Huffington Post, November 24, 2011, http://www.huffingtonpost.com/wallace-best-phd/the-misuse-of-langston-hughes_b_1024486.html.

Biemer, John. "Daniel Q. Posin, 93," Chicago *Tribune*. May 26, 2003,

http://articles.chicagotribune.com/2003-05-26/ news/0305260108_1_depaul-university-university-professor-physics.

Blair, Elizabeth. "The Strange Story of the Man Behind 'Strange Fruit'." *NPR Music*, http://www.npr.org/2012/09/05/158933012/the-strange-story-of-the-man-behind-strange-fruit, September 5, 2012.

Bontemps, Arna. *American Negro Poetry*. New York: Hill and Wang, 1963.

_____. au/ed. *American Negro Poetry, Revised Edition.* New York: Hill and Wang, 1975.

_____. au/ed. *American Negro Poetry.* St. Louis: Turtleback Books, 1995.

Bogue, Donald J., Anderton, Douglas L. and Barrett, Richard E. *The Population of the United States: 3rd Edition.* New York: Simon& Schuster, July 2010.

Boorstin, Daniel J. and Kelley, Brooks M. *A History of the United States.* Englewood Cliffs NJ: Prentice Hall, 1989.

Boston, Thomas D. "W. E. B. Du Bois and the Historical School of Economics." *The American Economic Review,* 81, No. 2, May 1991.

Bound, John and Turner, Sarah. "Going to War and Going to College: Did World War II and the G.I. Bill Increase Educational Attainment for Returning Veterans?" *Journal of Labor Economics.* 20, No. 4, October 2002.

"BPW to Hold 32nd Convention May 18-20." Bismarck *Tribune* (ND), May 10, 1951.

Brady, Sean. "All About Eve? Queer Theory and History," *Journal of Contemporary History.* 41, No.1, January 2006.

Bresciani, Dean L. "North Dakota State University State of the University Address," October 8, 2015.

https://www.ndsu.edu/president/speeches/stateoftheuniversityaddress2015/.

Brokaw, Tom. *The Greatest Generation.* New York: Random House, 2001.

Bruce. *New Georgia Encyclopedia.* online http://www.georgiaencyclopedia.org/articles/arts-culture/lillian-smith-1897-1966, September 1, 2015.

Buck v. Bell. 274 U.S.

"About CAU: History." *Clark Atlanta University.* http://www.cau.edu/about/cau-history.html.

California Death Index, 1940-1997. State of California. Sacramento, CA, USA: State of California Department of Health Services. Center for Health Statistics.

Cameron Brown, May. "The Language of Chaos: Quentin Compson in the Sound and the Fury." *American Literature,* 51, No. 4, January 1980.

Campus Office Directory, North Dakota State University. "Askanase Hall: Description." https://www.ndsu.edu/alphaindex/bioldings/Building::340.

Carroll, Charles. *The Negro a Beast.* St. Louis: American Book and Bible House, 1900.

_____. *The Tempter of Eve* (St. Louis: Adamic Publishing Co., 1902.

Catalogue of the Officers and Students of Atlanta University, 1909-1910. Atlanta: Atlanta University Press, Book 41. 1910.

The Catalogue 1912-1913. Atlanta: Atlanta University. The Atlanta University Bulletin, Atlanta University Catalogs, s. II no. 11, Book 43, 1913.

The Catalogue 1915-1916. Atlanta: Atlanta University. Atlanta University Catalogs.54, The Atlanta University Bulletin, s. II, no. 23, April 1916.

Cater, Catherine. "Contemporary Southern Writers." Thesis, Doctorate in English Language and Literature, University of Michigan, 1945.

____. Dr. Cater Speaks at Phi Kappa Phi Banquet." *Spectrum* (NDSU) May 13, 1960." File 33, Catherine Cater Collection, North Dakota State University Institute for Regional Studies & Universities Archives, Fargo, ND.

____. "Fire and Rock." 26th Faculty Lectureship Award Address, February 28, 1982, Box 1, File 34, Catherine Cater Collection. North Dakota State University Archives, Fargo, ND.

____. *Poetry Explorer.* Classic and Contemporary Poetry, Here And Now, By Catherine Cater. *http://www.poetryexplorer.net/poem.php?id=10047414.*

"Catherine Cater." Memorial Union Gallery (NDSU) Facebook Page. August 13, 2015.

Carvelle, Kevin. Letter to Robert Dodge. November 21, 2015.

"Celebrating Black History Month – Langston Hughes." *Center for African American Studies, Princeton University.* https://www.princeton.edu/africanamericanstudies/news/archive/index.xml?id=9594, Feb 12, 2014.

Tenth Census of the United States. 1880. Records of the Bureau of the Census. National Archives, Washington, Record Group 29. District 567, Henry, Georgia; Roll: 152; Family History Film: 1254152; Page: 240D; Enumeration District: 070; Image: 0483.

____. Seale, Russell, Alabama; Roll: 30; Family History Film: 1254030; Page: 577A; Enumeration District: 158; Image: 0557.

Twelfth Census of the United States, 1900. United States of America, Bureau of the Census. National Archives and Records Administration, Washington, D.C.: Census Place: *Atlanta Ward 4, Fulton, Georgia*; Roll: 199; Page: 2A; Enumeration District: 0063; FHL microfilm: 1240199.

Thirteenth Census of the United States. United States of America, Bureau of the Census. Washington, D.C.: National Archives and Records, *New Orleans Ward 14, Orleans, Louisiana*; Roll: T624_524; Page: 11B; Enumeration District: 0224; FHL microfilm: 1374537.

Fourteenth Census of the United States, 1920. United States Federal Census, Bureau of the Census. National Archives and Records Administration, Washington, D.C.: Census Place: Talladega Ward 2, Talladega, Alabama; Roll: T625_41; Page: 6A; Enumeration District: 136; Image: 796.

____. Record Group 29. Atlanta Ward 4, Fulton, Georgia; Roll: T625_250; Page: 19A; Enumeration District: 87; Image: 802.

Fifteenth Census of the United States, 1930. United States of America, Bureau of the Census. Washington, D.C.: National Archives and Records Administration, 1930. T626, 2,667 rolls, *Atlanta, Fulton, Georgia;* Roll: *361;* Page: *22B;* Enumeration District: *0059;* Image: *672.0;* FHL microfilm: *2340096*

____. Laurel, Jones, Mississippi; Roll: 1151; Page: 42A; Enumeration District: 0010; Image: 877.0; FHL microfilm: 2340886.

Sixteenth Census of the United States, 1940. United States of America, Bureau of the Census. Washington, D.C.: National Archives and Records Administration, 1940. T627, 4,643 rolls, *Talladega, Talladega, Alabama;* Roll: *T627_81;* Page: 22A; Enumeration District: 61-14.

____. T627, Atlanta, Fulton, Georgia; Roll: T627_726; Page: 9B; Enumeration District: 160-61.

Chaplin, Joyce E. "Creating a Cotton South in Georgia and South Carolina, 1760-1815." *The Journal of Southern History,* Vol. 57, No. 2, May, 1991.

"The Chinese Revolution of 1949." *Department of State, Office of the Historian.* https://history.state.gov/milestones/1945-1952/chinese-rev.

"Mr. Churchill's Address for United Effort for World Peace." *New York Times.* March 6, 1946.

Colby, Sandra L. and Ortman, Jennifer M. "The Baby Boom Cohort in the United States: 2012 to 2060, Current Population Reports." May 2014.

Constitution of the United States. Art. I, Sec. IX. para. 1.

Cook County Clerk, comp. *Cook County Clerk Genealogy Records.* Cook County Clerk's Office, Chicago, IL: Cook County Clerk, Marriage License, No. 1693478, filed August 7, 1951, 2008.

Condell, Yvonne. Interviewed by Robert Dodge. Moorhead, MN, October 11, 2015.

Cosgrove, William (Bill). Email to Robert Dodge. October 17, 2015.

____. Second Email to Robert Dodge. Oct 17, 2015.

Cox, John. Email to Robert Dodge. October 14, 2015.

Curtin, Philip D. *The Atlantic Slave Trade: A Census.* Madison, WI: University of Wisconsin Press, 1972.

"Daisy Cater." *Find A Grave.* http://www.findagrave.com/cgi-bin/fg.cgi

Dalfiume, Richard M. "The 'Forgotten Years' of the Negro Revolution." *The Journal of American History,* 55, No. 1, June 1968.

Danz, Greg. Interviewed by Robert Dodge. Fargo, ND, October 14, 2015.

Dell, George W. "Robert M. Hutchins' Philosophy of General Education and the College at the University of Chicago." *The Journal of General Education*, 30, No.1, Spring 1978.

"Demographics." *City of Fargo.* http://www.cityoffargo.com/CityInfo/Demographics.aspx.

Dictionary of American Scholars, Sixth Edition. Vol. 2: English, Speech, & Drama. New York: R.R. Bowker, 1974.

"Diseases and conditions: Vitiligo, *Mayo Clinic*, http://www.mayoclinic.org/diseases-conditions/vitiligo/basics/definition/con-20032007.

Disrud, Stephen. Interviewed by Robert Dodge. Fargo, ND, October 13, 2015.

Dodge, Robert. *Andrea and Sylvester.* New York: Algora Publishing, 2015.

____. *Prairie Murders*, North Star Press, St. Cloud, MN: 2009.

Donohue, William A. *The Politics of the American Civil Liberties Union.* Piscataway, NJ: Transaction Publishers, 1985.

Dura, Jack. " 'A Helluva Good Time in Zap, North Dakota': From 1969's Zip to Zap to 2015, Spring Break Safety as Important as Ever" *Spectrum.* http://ndsuspectrum.com/a-helluva-good-time-in-zap-north-dakota/ March 12, 2015.

Ehrman, John. "A Half-Century of Controversy: The Alger Hiss Case," *Central Intelligence Agency.* https://www.cia.gov/library/center-for-the-study-of-intelligence/kent-csi/vol44no5/html/v44i5a01p.htm.

"Endymion, Greek Mythology." *Encyclopedia Britannica.* http://www.britannica.com/topic/Endymion-Greek-mythology.

"Endymion." http://www.bartleby.com/126/32/html.

Ericksmoen, Curk. "Fargo Native a Big Success in Business." Bismarck *Tribune*, April 4, 2010.

Estate of Allan Bradford Monks, Deceased. Ida Nancy Lee et al. V. Antoinette Giraudo. Civ. No. 2832. Fourth Dist. December 19, 1941.

"Excerpts: Catherine Cater," *NDSU Magazine.* Vol. 01, No.1, Fall, 2000. Catherine Cater Collection, Box 1, Folder 37, North Dakota State University Archives, Fargo, ND.

Executive Order 8802: "Prohibition of Discrimination in the Defense Industry." *National Archives.* http://www.archives.gov/historical-docs/todays-doc/?dod-date=625.

"Executive Order 9981: Desegregation of the Armed Forces (1948)." www.ourdocuments.gov/doc.php?doc=84.

Faulkner, William. *The Sound and the Fury.* New York: Jonathan Cape and Harrison Smith, 1929.

"Fergus Falls Civic Orchestra Spring Concert: Soloist – James Condell." *Daily Journal* (Fergus Falls, MN). April 6, 1973.

Ferber, Marianne A and Loeb, Jane W. *Academic Couples: Problems and Promises.* Urbana: University of Illinois Press, 1997.

Ferrell, Robert H. "The Last Hurrah." *The Wilson Quarterly*, 12, No. 2, Spring 1988.

"Find a Grave: Daisy Cater," http://www.findagrave.com/cgibin/fg.cgi?page=gsr&GSln=Cater&GSiman=1&GScid=35955&.

Finding Aid to the Catherine Cater Papers. "Biography." Catherine Cater Collection, North Dakota State University Institute for Regional Studies & Universities Archives, Fargo, ND.

Freedman, Lawrence D. "Frostbitten: Decoding the Cold War, 20 Years Later," *Foreign Affairs.* 89, No.2, March/April 2010.

Gartrell, Dan. *A Guidance Approach for the Encouraging Classroom.* Belmont, CA: Wadsworth Publishing Co, 2013.

Gaynor, Peggy. Interviewed on telephone by Robert Dodge. November 21, 2015.

"GE College Bowl TV Show History." http://www.collegebowl.com/schoolhistoryrpt.asp?CustomerID=252.

"General Declaration, Customs, Immigration, and Public Health." Northwest Airlines Inc., Aircraft No 74601, Flight No. 702. September 1, 1951.

"Georgia Deaths, 1914–1927." *FamilySearch.* Georgia Department of Health and Vital Statistics, Atlanta, Georgia.

"Georgia Deaths, 1930." *FamilySearch.* Georgia Department of Health and Vital Statistics, Atlanta, Georgia.

Glaser, Emily. "The Song of the Century: Billie Holiday's 'Strange Fruit'." *PorterBriggs.Com: The Voice of the South*, http://porterbriggs.com/billie-holiday-strange-fruit/.

Glass, Andrew. "Congress Votes to Ban Slave Trade: March 2, 1807," *Politico.* http://www.politico.com/story/2009/03/congress-votes-to-ban-slave-trade-march-2-1807-019465, March 2, 2009.

Goldin, Claudia and Shim, Maria. "Making a Name: Women's Surnames at Marriage and Beyond," *The Journal of Economic Perspectives.* 18, No. 2, Spring 2004.

Goldstein, Robert Justin. "Prelude to McCarthyism: The Making of a Blacklist." National Archives, 38, No. 3, Fall 2006, http://www.archives.gov/publications/prologue/2006/fall/agloso.html.

Golightly, Cornelius. "Negro Morale in Boston." Special Services Division Report No. 7, May 19, 1942.

____. "Negro Organizations and the War Effort." Report from the Special Services Division. Submitted April 23, 1942.

"Golightly, Cornelius L., 1917–1976: Biography, Civil Rights Digital Library: Documenting America's Struggle for Racial Equality." http://crdl.usg.edu/people/g/golightly_cornelius_l_1917_1976/?Welcome.

"Dr. Cornelius Golightly (1917–1976): The Life of an Academic and Public Intellectual." BlackPast.org. http://www.blackpast.org/perspectives/dr-cornelius-golightly-1917-1976-life-academic-and-public-intellectual.

Goodman, Bonnie K. "1948: Presidential Campaign & Elections." https://presidentialcampaignselectionsreference.wordpress.com/overviews/20th-century/1948-overview/.

Goldman, Eric F. *The Crucial Decade – And After: America, 1945-1960.* New York: Alfred A. Knopf, 1960.

Grant, Donald. *The Way It Was in the South: The Black Experience in Georgia.* Athens, GA: University of Georgia Press, 2001.

"Guest Professors." *Pittsburgh Courier.* August 2, 1947.

Gunnels Rush, Theressa, Fairbanks Myers, Carol and Spring Arata, Esther. *Black American Writers Past and Present: A Biographical and Bibliographical Dictionary.* Metuchen, NJ: Scarecrow Press, 1975.

Haga, Chuck. "Some Who Zipped to Zap Will Gather Again." Minnpost, https://www.minnpost.com/politics-policy/2009/05/some-who-zipped-zap-will-gather-again, May 5, 2009.

Hamby, Alonzo L. "1948 Democratic Convention: The South Secedes Again." *Smithsonian Magazine,* Aug 2008, www.smithsonianmag.com/.../1948-democratic-convention-.

Hanson, Nancy Edmonds. "Catherine Cater: Her Former Students at Moorhead State and NDSU Repeatedly Describe Her as 'A Great Teacher'," *Howard Binford's Guide to Fargo, Moorhead, and West Fargo* 15, No. 3, September 1983. Box 1, File 19, Catherine Cater Collection, North Dakota State University Archives, Fargo, ND.

Harley, Sharon. *Sister Circle: Black Women and Work.* New Brunswick, NJ: Rutgers University Press, 2002.

Hawley, Lourdes. Interviewed by telephone by Robert Dodge. November 25, 2015.

Hickman, Christine B. "The Devil and the One Drop Rule: Racial Categories, African Americans, and the U.S. Census." *Michigan Law Review,* 95, No. 5, March 1997.

"History." United States Census Bureau. https://www.census.gov/history/www/through_the_decades/index_of_questions/1900_1.html

"History Essay Prize Won by Former Cotton Picker." New York *Age*. December 9, 1939.

Hogue, Fred. "Social Eugenics," Los Angeles *Times*. July 5, 1936.

Holliday, Billie. "Strange Fruit." https://www.youtube.com/watch?v= 0mO92ll_q0k.

Holmquist. Delsie. "Speech about Catherine Cater, to NDSU Blue Key Fraternity Banquet, for Blue Key Doctor of Service Award, 1970." File 44, Catherine Cater Collection, North Dakota State University Institute for Regional Studies & Universities Archives, Fargo, ND.

Homan, Paul. "A Humanist in Honors: Another Look at Catherine Cater." *Journal of the National Collegiate Honors Council*, Paper 193, http://digitalcommons.unl.edu/nchcjournal/193, Fall/Winter, 2000.

_____. Interviewed by Robert Dodge. Fargo, ND, October 13, 2015.

Hornblower, Simon. *The Oxford Classical Dictionary*. Oxford University Press, Oxford, UK: 2005.

Horowitz, Irving Louis and Bramson, Victoria Curtis. "Skokie, the ACLU and the Endurance of Democratic Theory." *Law and Contemporary Problems*, 43, No. 2, Spring 1979.

Huebner, Robin. "Communiversity Celebrates 50th Year of Learning." Fargo *Forum* online, http:www.onforum.com/news/education/3674565-communiversity-celebrates-50th –year-learning, February 8, 2015.

Hughes, Langston. "Langston Hughes: a Biography." *Masterpiece Theatre/ American Collection/Cora Unashamed*. http://www.pbs.org/wgbh/masterpiece/americancollection/cora/ei_hughesbiography.html.

_____. *The Big Sea: An Autobiography*. New York: Hill and Wang, 2015.

_____. *Fine Clothes to the Jew*. New York: A. A. Knoff, 1929.

Hughes, Langston and Bontemps, Arna. *The Poetry of the Negro*. Garden City, New York: Doubleday & Company, 1951.

Hutchins, Robert Maynard. *The Higher Learning in America*. New Haven: Yale University Press, 1936.

"The Immigration Act of 1924 (The Jonson-Reed Act)." U.S. Department of State Office of the Historian. http://history.state.gov/milestones/19211936/ImmigrationAct.

Inscoe. John C. "Killers of the Dream," *New Georgia Encyclopedia*. http://www.georgiaencyclopedia.org/articles/arts-culture/killers-dream, Aug 22, 2013.

Jackson, John P. and Weidman, Nadine M. "The Origins of Scientific Racism." *The Journal of Blacks in Higher Education*, No. 50, Winter 2005/2006.

"John Maynard Hutchins: American Educator." *Encyclopedia Britannica*. http://www.britannica.com/biography/Robert-Maynard-Hutchins.

Johnson, Merle. "Wonderful Memories of Great Teachers." letter, Fargo *Forum*, September 11, 2015.

Johnson, Kevin R. *Mixed Race and the Law*. New York: NYU Press, 2003.

"JSU History." *Jackson State University*. http://www.jsums.edu/unite/jsu-history/.

Kennedy, David M. *Freedom from Fear: The American People in Depression and War 1929-1945*. New York: Oxford University Press, 1999.

Kidd, Colin. *The Forging of Races: Race and Scripture in the Protestant Atlantic World, 1600–2000*. Cambridge, UK: Cambridge University Press, 2006.

Kirkpatrick, Rob. *1969: The Year Everything Changed*. New York: Skyhorse Publishing, 2011.

Kosse, Ellen. "Cater: 'infect one another with the desire to learn,' " *Spectrum* (North Dakota State University), Feb 8, 1977. Box 1, Folder 17, Catherine Cater Collection, North Dakota State University Archives, Fargo, ND.

"Ku Klux Klan - Facts & Summary - HISTORY.com." *History*. http://www.history.com/topics/ku-klux-klan.

"A Landing a Day: Zap, North Dakota." https://landingaday.wordpress.com/tag/zip-to-zap/.

Larew, Don. Interviewed by Robert Dodge. Fargo, ND, October 12, 2015.

Lawrence, W.H. "Truman, Barkley Named by Democrats; South Loses on Civil Rights, 35 Walk Out; President Will Recall Congress July 26." New York *Times*, July 15, 1948.

Leeming. David. *The Oxford Companion to World Mythology*. New York: Oxford University Press, 2005.

Lennig, Arthur. "Myth and Fact: The Reception of 'The Birth of a Nation'." *Film History*, 16, No. 2, 2004.

Lester, A Hoyle. *The Pre-Adamite, or Who Tempted Eve*. Philadelphia: J.B. Lippincott, 1875.

"The Library of Kevin: One Man's Quest to Archive North Dakota's Literary Landscape in His House." *NDSU Magazine*. Spring 2007.

Lippmann, Walter. *The Cold War: A Study in U.S. Foreign Policy*. New York: Harper Brothers, 1947.

Lyons, Reneé Critcher. "The Second Shall Be First: 1948 Presidential Election – Truman V. Dewey, *Our White House: Looking In, Looking Out*. http://www.ourwhitehouse.org/secondshallbefirst.html.

Martinez, James Michael. *Carpetbaggers, Cavalry, and the Ku Klux Klan: Exposing the Invisible Empire During Reconstruction*. Lanham, MD: Rowman & Littlefield, 2007.

McCormick, J. Scott. "The Julius Rosenwald Fund," *The Journal of Negro Education*. 3, No. 4, October 1934.

"McGrath's Statement to the House Committee on Un-American Activities." *Modern American Poetry*. http://www.english.illinois.edu/maps/poets/m_r/mcgrath/huac.htm.

McNair, Glenn. *Criminal Injustice: Slaves and Free Blacks in Georgia's Criminal Justice System.* Charlottesville, VA: University of Virginia Press, 2009.

McDaniel, Laura. Email to Robert Dodge. October 13, 2015.

McNeese, Tim. American Colonies. Dayton, OH: Lorenz Educational Press, 2002.

Meier, August and Lewis, David. "History of the Negro Upper Class in Atlanta, Georgia, 1890-1958." *The Journal of Negro Education*, 28, No. 2, Spring 1959.

Memorial Union Gallery Collections, Object ID: M159, www.ndsu.edu/mu/programs/gallery/collections/.

Michigan Christian Advocate. Detroit: Michigan Christian Advocate Publishing Company. 75, 1948.

"Mission." *National Collegiate Honors Association.* http://nchchonors.org.

Mohr, Clarence L. *On The Threshold of Freedom: Masters and Slaves in Civil War Georgia.* Baton Rouge, LA: LSU Press, 2001.

Montagu, Ashley. *Man's Most Dangerous Myth: The Fallacy of Race.* New York: Harpers, 1942.

Morrissey, Mike. Interviewed by Robert Dodge. Fargo, ND, October 9, 2015.

Morton, Patricia. "From Invisible Man to 'New People': The Recent Discovery of American Mulattoes," *Phylon*, 46, No. 2, 2nd Quarter, 1985.

Motomura, Hiroshi. "Whose Alien Nation?: Two Models of Constitutional Immigration Law," *Michigan Law Review*. 94, No. 6, May 1996.

Nassaw, David. "Show-Stopper: Strange Fruit: Billie Holiday, Café Society, and an Early Cry for Civil Rights," *New York Times*, May 21, 2000.

National Archives and Records Administration. Year: 1946; Arrival: *Gripsholm* manifest, New York, New York. Microfilm Serial: T715, 1897-1957; Microfilm Roll: Roll 7169.

"Negro Teacher Weds White Coed." *Jet.* January 10, 1952.

Neumaier, John. Moorhead State University Archives, Moorhead, MN. https://www.mnstate.edu/university-archives/125th-anniversary/1960s/.

"NDSU Historical Facts." North Dakota State University Archives. http://library.ndsu.edu/ndsuarchives/ndsu-historical-facts.

"NDSU Faculty Lecture Centers on Durable Myths." Fargo *Forum*. March 1, 1982.

"NDSU Shares Its Act Collection Via the Internet," https://www.ndsu.edu/news/banner_stories/digitalgallery/, November 14, 2013.

"The Night President Teddy Roosevelt Invited Booker T. Washington to Dinner." *The Journal of Blacks in Higher Education*. No. 35 Spring 2002.

Nowatzki, Mike. " Tri-College to Celebrate 35th Anniversary: Founding Member George Sinner Retires From Board." Fargo *Forum*. July 6, 2004.

Olson, Keith W. "The G. I. Bill and Higher Education: Success and Surprise." *American Quarterly*. 25, No. 5. December 1973.

Olson, Dave. "Former Clay County Judge Helps Rebuild Justice in Kosovo." Fargo *Forum* online, April 12, 2010.

"Our History." *Olivet College*. http://www.olivetcollege.edu/content/our-history.

Owram, Doug. *Born at the Right Time: A History of the Baby Boom Generation*. Toronto: University of Toronto Press, 1997.

Pace v Alabama. 106 US 583. 1882.

Payne, Buckner H 'Ariel.' *The Negro: What Is His Ethnological Status*. Cincinnati: self published, 1867.

Papadopoulos, Linda, Bor, Robert and Legg, Charles. "Coping With the Disfiguring Effects of Vitiligo: A Preliminary Investigation into the Effects of Cognitive-Behavioural Therapy," *British Journal of Medical Psychology*. 72. 1999.

Parker, A. Warner. "The Ineligible to Citizenship Provisions of the Immigration Act of 1924," *The American Journal of International Law*. January 1925.

Pascoe, Peggy. "Miscegenation Law, Court Cases, and Ideologies of 'race' in Twentieth-century America." *The Journal of American History*, 83, No. 1. June 1996.

____. *What Comes Naturally*. New York: Oxford University Press, 2010.

Perleberg, Jeremy. "Thomas McGrath: Politics and Poetry." *Horisonslines.org*, http://www.horizonlines.org/Volume1/inprint/mcgrath.html.

Pinkney, Gene P. "She Was a Brilliant Teacher Who Taught Us How to Think." letter, Fargo *Forum*, August 23, 2015.

Plessy v. Ferguson. 163 US 537. 1896.

Pollard, C.A. letter to Cater, Catherine. July 27, 1948. Box 1, Folder 37, Catherine Cater Collection, North Dakota State University (NDSU) Institute for Regional Studies & Universities Archives, Fargo, ND.

Print Material Series, 7/7, 7/8. Finding Aid to the NDSU Development Foundation Records, NDSU Institute for Regional Studies & Universities Archives, Fargo, ND. http://library.ndsu.edu/repository/bitstream/handle/10365/395/DevelopmentFoundation-Records.pdf.

"Professor Ralph Engle Scholarship." https://www.ndsu.edu/english/ourprogram/.

"Radio and Television Report to the American People on the Soviet Arms Buildup in Cuba, October 22, 1962." John F Kennedy Presidential Library and Museum. http://www.jfklibrary.org/Asset-Viewer/sU-VmCh-sB0moLfrBcaHaSg.aspx.

Randolph, Laura B. "The NAACP Turns 80." *Ebony*, 44, No. 9, July 1989.

"The Red Scare." *History*. http://www.history.com/topics/cold-war/red-scare.

Richardson, Lou and Jerry. Interviewed together by Robert Dodge. Fargo, ND, October, 9, 2015.

Richardson, Jerry. "Dr. Catherine Cater & The Life of the Mind." Unpublished manuscript.

____. Telephone interview by Robert Dodge. November 17, 2015.

Richardson, Seth W. and Truman, Harry S. "The Federal Employee Loyalty Program." *Columbia Law Review*, 51, No. 5, May 1951.

Riley, Thomas. Email to Robert Dodge. October 15, 2015.

Rogin, Michael. " 'The Sword Became a Flashing Vision': D.W. Griffin's The Birth of a Nation," *Representations*. No. 9, Winter 1985.

Robinson, Elwyn B. *History of North Dakota*. Lincoln: University of Nebraska Press, 1966.

Rubin, Edward L. "Review: Nazis, Skokie, and the First Amendment as Virtue." *California Law Review*, 74, No. 1, January 1986.

Sarburn, Josh. "Strange Fruit." *Time* online, Oct 21, 2011.

Satel, Sally. "A Better Breed of American," New York *Times*. February 26, 2006.

Savage, Sean J. "To Purge or Not to Purge: Hamlet Harry and the Dixiecrats, 1948-1952," *Presidential Studies Quarterly*. 27, No. 4, Fall 1997.

Schlesinger Jr., Arthur M. *A Thousand Days: John F. Kennedy in the White House*. New York: Mariner Books, 2002.

Sealing, Keith. "Blood Will Tell: Scientific Racism and the Legal Prohibition Against Miscegenation." SSRN 1260015, 2000 - papers.ssrn.com, 2000.

To Secure These Rights. Harry S Truman Library and Museum. www.blackpast.org/african-american-history-primary-documents.

Selden, Steven. "Transforming Better Babies into Fitter Families: Archival Resources and the History of the American Eugenics Movement, 1908-1930," *Proceedings of the American Philosophical Society*. 149, No. 2, June 2005.

Shenk, Conor. "All in the Name of Learning," *Spectrum* (North Dakota State University) November 3, 2000. Folder 22, Catherine Cater Collection, North Dakota State University Institute for Regional Studies & Universities Archives, Fargo, ND.

Shropshire, Kenneth L. "Where Have You Gone, Jackie Robinson?: Integration in America in the 21st Century." *South Texas Law Review*, 38.

Sitkoff, Harvard. "Harry Truman and the Election of 1948: The Coming of Age of Civil Rights in American Politics." *The Journal of Southern History*, 27, No. 4, November 1971.

Slayton, Robert A. "When a Catholic Terrified the Heartland." *New York Times*, October 10, 2011.

Smith Booklist. "Strange Fruit Book Review," Summary.

Smith, Lillian. *Strange Fruit*. New York: Reynal & Hitchcock, 1944.

____. *Killers of the Dream*. New York: W.W. Norton, 1949.

Snarr, Otto Welton. "Biographical Note." 1886 - 1966. Collection, 1857 – 1968, Minnesota State University, Mankato, Memorial Library, Southern Minnesota Historical Center.

"Sold on Song: Strange Fruit." *BBC*. http://www.bbc.co.uk/radio2/soldonsong/songlibrary/indepth/strangefruit.shtml.

Sollors, Werner. *Interracialism: Black-White Intermarriage in American History, Literature, and Law*. New York: Oxford University Press, 2000.

"Souvenirs Donated to NDSU." Grand Forks *Herald* (ND). November 19, 2000.

Sova, Dawn B. *Literature Suppressed on Social Grounds*. New York: Facts on File, 2006.

Special Correspondent. "Complete Restoration of the State – New State Government – Gen. Smith's Inaugural – The United States Senatorship." *New York Tribune*, July 20, 1868.

Stanley, Marcus. "College Education and the Midcentury GI Bills," *The Quarterly Journal of Economics*, 118, No. 2, May 2003.

"State Coat of Arms." North Dakota.gov. http://www.nd.gov/content.htm?parentCatID=74&id=State%20Coat%20of%20Arms.

State of Georgia, *Indexes of Vital Records for Georgia: Deaths, 1919-1998*. Georgia, USA: Georgia Health Department, Office of Vital Records, 1998.

Stern, Fredrick C. "A Biographical Sketch of Thomas McGrath." *Modern American Poetry,* http://www.english.illinois.edu/maps/poets/m_r/mcgrath/life.htm.

Stern, Sheldon M. *The Week the World Stood Still: Inside the Secret Cuban Missile Crisis.* Palo Alto, CA: Stanford University Press, 2004.

Stocker, Pat. Email to Robert Dodge. November 18, 2015.

Stokes, Mason. *The Color of Sex: Whiteness, Heterosexuality, and the Fictions of White Supremacy.* Durham, N.C, Duke University Press, 2001.

____. "Someone's in the Garden with Eve: Race, Religion, and the American Fall," *American Quarterly,* 50, No. 4, December 1998.

Stone, Geoffrey R. "Free Speech in the Age of McCarthy: A Cautionary Tale," *California Law Review.* 93, No. 5, October 2005.

"Starwars.com 10: Best Yoda Quotes," *Star Wars,* http://www.starwars.com/news/the-starwars-com-10-best-yoda-quotes.

Star Wars. http://www.starwars.com/databank/yoda.

St. Martinville, LA. Box 1, file 2, Catherine Cater Collection, North Dakota State University (NDSU) Institute for Regional Studies & Universities Archives, Fargo, ND.

"Strange Fruit:1939," *The Pop History Dig.* http://www.pophistorydig.com/topics/tag/billie-holiday-1940s/.

Svalesen, Leif. *The Slave Ship Fredensborg.* Bloomington, IND: Indiana University Press, 2000.

"Talladega College History," *Talladega College.* http://www.talladega.edu/history.asp.

Taylor, Carol M. "W.E.B. DuBois's Challenge to Scientific Racism." *Journal of Black Studies.* 11, No. 4, June 1981.

Taylor, Quintard. *In Search of the Racial Frontier: African Americans in the American West 1528-1990.* New York: ☐W. W. Norton, 1999.

The Trans-Atlantic Slave Trade Database. http://www.slavevoyages.org/tast/index.faces.

"Thomas McGrath; Poet Was Blacklisted in '50s," Los Angeles *Times,* September 24, 1990.

Traub, Valerie. "The Present Future of Lesbian Historiography." http://www.mcgill.ca/files/igsf/PresentFutureofLesbianHistoriography.pdf.

Tri-College University. https://www.tri-college.org/about_tcu/history_of_tcu/June10.

"Truman's Democratic Convention Acceptance Speech: July 15, 1948." www.pbs.org/newshour/spc/character/links/truman_speech.html.

Truman, Harry S. "In Korean Crisis." *Life,* February 6, 1956.

Tuchman, Arleen Marcia. "Diabetes and Race, a Historical Perspective." *American Journal of Public Health*, 101, No.1, January 2011.

University of Michigan: The President's Report for 1938-1939. Ann Arbor, MI: University of Michigan, University of Michigan Official Publication, Ann Arbor, MI: University of Michigan Libraries.

U.S. Supreme Court. Pace v. Alabama, 106 U.S. 583 (1883). https://supreme.justia.com/cases/federal/us/106/583/.

Vanorny, Hannah. Taped interview of Catherine Cater, two tapes, A and B, and "Interview Synopsis," April 13, 2005. Box 1, File 7, Catherine Cater Collection, North Dakota State University Archives, Fargo, ND.

Vogel, Ene Kõivastik. Telephone interview with Robert Dodge. November 18, 2015.

Ward, Steve. Interviewed by Robert Dodge. Fargo, ND, October 11, 2015.

Who's Who Of The Colored Race V1, 1915: A General Biographical Dictionary Of Men And Women Of African Descent, Volume One. Fort Wayne, IN, U.S.A: Hyde Brothers, Booksellers. 1915.

Wood, Forrest G. *Black Scare: The Racist Response to Emancipation and Reconstruction.* Berkeley: University of California Press, 1968.

World War I Selective Service System Draft Registration Cards, 1917-1918. United States, Selective Service System. Louisiana; Registration County: Orleans; Roll: 1684818; Draft Board: 02, National Archives and Records Administration, Washington, D.C.

____. *Georgia;* Registration County: *Fulton;* Roll: *1556947;* Draft Board: *4,* National Archives and Records Administration. M1509, 4,582 rolls, Washington, D.C.

____. National Archives and Records Administration, M1509, Mississippi; Registration County: Marshall; Roll: 1682940.

Yancy, George. *Reframing the Practice of Philosophy: Bodies of Color, Bodies of Knowledge.* Albany, NY: SUNY Press, 2012.

"Young Negro Student Wins $300.00 Award: Takes 1st Prize in National Contest; University of Michigan Student Shows Qualities in Contest." *Pittsburgh Courier.* December 23, 1939.

INDEX